# The Passion of Life: Escaping the Holocaust

D1606524

Helene J. RW. Wald

REGISTRATION NUMBER-TXu 2-228-109

Library of Congress Control Number: 2018675309

Printed in the United States of America

ISBN: 979-8-5826-4481-1

# DEDICATION

I dedicate this book in honor of the Lord, who has protected me till this day.
This book is dedicated to all my family, my parents, my first husband Maurice ,my daughter ,grandson and great-granddaughter. And all my friends, who touched my heart

And to all the righteous people all over the world, who practice Tikkun Olam.
To Howard, my current husband, who helped me so much to accomplish this task.

# Table of Contents

# Prologue

The question that I always ask myself: why some of the people called human beings seem to only take pleasure, in the destruction of things and people? Yes already 58 years old and still I never changed. My passion for everything, wisdom, caution, I don't know about. Excessive in everything and the difficulties in life, did not teach me it. So far as I remember, my passion started many dramas. When I was a little girl, being very timid and lacking self confidence, for a yes or a no. But as the years went on, the passion overwhelmed everything. When I am angry, I feel like a volcano, ready to explode. Normally I am not aggressive, but if somebody is looking for me, they will find me. My brother-in-law said that it's like I go up to the front, as in a war. My temperament should bring me many enemies, but usually people like me. I have real relationships with people. I push them to the wall and try to get the best of their spirit. The same passion pushed me to discover the real nature of people. I am not interested in the superficial nature of people. It's the deep nature of everyone that I am looking to find. But it is very difficult, because people always have a barrier to hide behind. Of course, what is the most important is being sincere. You have to make yourself naked, and not be afraid to talk about your feelings, fear and happiness. Almost 6 months have passed since I wrote this line; the routine of life took me away from expressing my thoughts and remembering my past. It took me away from telling the story of all the people who contributed to what I am today. When I was a young girl, at the time when a young girl thinks about playing with dolls, I discovered that the worst enemy of mankind was human beings. And that they were capable of the worst. In the front of G-d, I was ashamed of humanity. How human beings can humiliate their fellows, and suppress their dignity. It's a negation of other peoples, and your own downfall. It's in the respect of everyone, that you elevate yourself. Accomplishing a good deed, gives you so much happiness. To give and make happy another human being is easy, to cultivate a little happiness everyday. When you have a full life and comes the time to leave this world, then you can have some tenderness for yourself, thinking that the people will eternally regret you. The war, the torture, destroys what the others built. Maybe it's a way to convince themselves of their power over people, deciding life and death like G-d. Knowing that people are mortal themselves, they want to destroy the maximum before they pass away. They start by destroying their own souls. And the more evil they can accomplish. They arrive to disguise themselves, the torturers, as the victims. And their victims, as the guilty ones, accusing them of all the evils of the earth. This way, the Nazi's accuse the poor Jews, to be responsible for the cataclysm that they caused. The poor Jews stunned, end up themselves to believe they are guilty. Since the rest of the world was a witness to their destruction, and did not seem to care about it. Myself, at this time, I thought that the Jews were responsible for the death of Jesus. And only later I realized that Jesus was Jewish also! And that he was tortured like other Jews by the Romans, the Nazi's of that time period. Again to justify their crimes, they accuse the Jew to be the instigator of the death and crucifixion of Jesus. For my belief is that G-d created Adam with love in his image, and created Eve to fill in his loneliness and to give life, for sharing the joy. Only death cannot be shared, because when you die human beings are alone facing G-d. Maybe death is the immortality, because the ones who pass away, nothing can affect them. Not the sadness, not the illness, not the pleasures. They are eternal in their silence and us happy mortals, we carry with us all the anguish of what can happen to us tomorrow. When you love somebody, and this one disappears after much suffering, you feel relief, because nothing can reach them.

# 1 Childhood

My parents emigrated from Poland and arrived in France in 1928, thinking that everything was going to be wonderful from then on in sweet France, but they were quickly disabused of their illusions. They had to work hard to make a living. They were both, I just realized, in the flower of their youth, both in their twenties. My father had had a hard time convincing my mother to make the trip to France. They had known each other in Poland since childhood, for they lived in the same courtyard in Lotz, the textile capital, a fact which had a lasting impact on their lives, for they remained their entire lives in the garment business.

My mother had a very good reputation. She came from a family of ten children. Her father died when she was very young, and she had to work from the age of 14 in order to help support the family. When my father first set his heart on her, she didn't even look at him. A serious young woman, she did not permit boys to get too close to her. If they did, they received a punch below the stomach, which, it seems, hurt a good deal.

My father drove a wagon with a horse to deliver merchandise. He was a good looking man with blond hair, beautiful blue eyes, an aquiline nose, not Jewish looking with high cheekbones; all-in-all hopelessly charming. The conquering male heart throb, for whom all the girls swooned, knew no rest until my mother agreed to go out with him. This was the origin of the great French adventure. My ambitious father wanted to escape from the mediocrity of his situation, and chomping at the bit like a young colt, he saw no future for himself in a Poland that was both backward and anti-Semitic. More than once he had had to prove his right to exist by using his fists against gangs of Poles.

My mother had brown hair, green eyes, a small turned-up nose, and was a beautiful women. My father left first; as his final job in Poland had been as a cap maker, he hoped to conquer the French market. The advantage of this job is that your work tool is a small sewing machine, hardly higher than three apples stacked on top of each other and which you can easily carry under your arm. If you have a problem with the boss, you can leave with your equipment without any problem. My father who did not have a particularly docile nature often had problems with his bosses.

2

My mother, on the other hand, had nimble fingers, and she found work immediately. Thus it was the good fortune of this future family that the daily bread would be reliably provided thanks to my mother.

After having begun their new existence in a seedy hotel room on the rue Vercingetorix, they were soon able to rent a room. It was a luxury to have one's own place and it allowed me to make my entrance into the world. The situation was not entirely sunny, for my mother could not even contemplate quitting her job. She was the gold mine for the family, and thus she brought me along to the workshop and home of her Aunt and Uncle. I was allowed to share the bed of my little cousin David, it seems that I was adorable and in no way disturbed the activities of the clothing workshop, where my mother did the job of attaching sleeves, a job at which she excelled.

During this period my father was seeking his way in life, from one cap workshop to the next, improving his French considerably as he associated with real Frenchmen in these work shops, whereas my mother used mostly Yiddish in her family milieu. My father developed his French and even lost his Polish accent. As a result of an unclear episode in my life, my father left with his friends to travel around France in order to learn about things, while my mother was alone with me.

It was at that time that a first cousin of my mother (the most wealthy branch of the family), who had emigrated from Poland to America, came to Paris. She and my mother were very close, and seeing my mother's situation, she wanted to bring the two of us to America. Unfortunately my mother loved terra firma and could not countenance the idea of getting on a boat, and that is why I, a little girl from Polish immigrants, remained French rather than becoming American. This must have been in 1931 or 1932. How can one know whether a decision is good or bad? Only the future reveals what was the best. Then, after trying his luck all over France and Navarre, my father came back home full of ideas.

Seeing that he had no future prospects working for bosses, he decided to become his own boss, and the nimble fingers of his wife would become his bonanza and not that of others. The American cousin had left a nice sum of money for her cousin. That sum served to obtain a two-room apartment (a great luxury for them) in the Passage St. Bernard where my father was able to start a business making boxer shorts, an article of clothing important to masculine comfort. My first childhood memory comes from that place. I see myself sitting on the steps of that building with a little boy whose name I do not remember, but with who I was already, at four years of age, very much in love. I still recall that first love and disappointment. My father, restless yet again, decided that we needed to improve our lodgings and moved us to an apartment with an exorbitantly high rent on the Avenue Ledru-Rollin, ostensibly for the sake of my mother. What a madman! At four thousand francs a year, it surely spelled our ruin. She had to work day and night just to pay the rent. But it was clear she had to go along with my father's plans, for he had character and ambition, and he reproached my mother for her lack of enthusiasm at the idea of improving their social and financial standing. My mother, with her good sense, understood that for every rung one climbed on the social ladder, one had to sweat blood and water, and she foresaw the sleepless nights that awaited her.

My last memories of the Passage St. Bernard include a tonsil operation. I have a horrible recollection of being on a virtual assembly line in the Rothschild hospital, one behind another. With a pair of pincers they ripped out a tonsil that they then threw into a little basin, and the next child in line had this blood-stained image before their eyes. Then they began all over again for the second go-around. I struggled with all my might on this second time, and three of them were not able to hold me still. Given that the treatment was free and they were tired of fighting me, they let me go home with one large tonsil and the other one removed. To this day I feel a certain pain in my mouth that prevents me from sucking ice cubes.

I was on a deck chair of rattan. This is the last memory I have of that apartment. My father had taken in a dog of the same breed as Ric and Rac that someone left at our doorstep one evening. The dog took his revenge for being abandoned by tearing up the rolls of jersey that were used to make the long and short undergarments. My father took the dog to the Bois de Vincennes in order to abandon it there, but this dog that was clever, found his way back to our apartment. It must be noted that my mother detested dogs, but she was incapable of harming a flea, and since my father imposed the dog on her, the animal was well cared for.

He was a typical dog and we could not leave him alone in the house. I remember one beautiful summer evening at the Place de la Bastille: this adorable animal, whether out of jealousy or madness, took a bite out of my dress and pulled out the entire lining. He thereby signed his own death warrant. My father took him on his racing bike 50 kilometers outside of Paris and we thought we were rid of him for good. But two days later, there he was, once again at our door. I never learned how exactly the story ended, but my father took drastic measures and thus ended the passionate love that this dog felt for us. As strongly as my mother hated dogs, my father loved them, and his life is dotted with episodes involving dogs. Let me say straight out that my father was right to move to the apartment on the Avenue Ledru-Rollin which looked out on the courtyard Hermel; it was spacious and airy, with several workshops.

# 2  Quiet before the Storm

1935: move to Ledru-Rollin, enrolment in kindergarten on rue Charles Baudelaire. I interrupted the writing of my memories for more than a year. I have just reread all that I wrote. I have lost my great optimism, because my mother has been added to the list of those I have lost forever. I will never forget what she said on October 16, 1989: "I have never in my entire life suffered as much as this, and I can't go on." She is the only person I have ever seen pass from life to death. It happened so quickly and yet at the same time seemed so mysterious. I will try to go on from where I left off.

1937. My father had suffered for years from a stomach ulcer. I often saw him rolling on the ground in agony when he had one of his attacks. He made up his mind to undergo an operation to be performed bythe professor Leibovici at the Butte Chaumont hospital. At that time the operation in question was an achievement. I recall visiting my father at that hospital which was situated high up and from where one could see all of Paris. His business had grown, and he managed to set up a workshop right under our apartment that employed a dozen workers, of which my mother was the irreplaceable sewing machinist. I recall a very pleasant ambiance, laughter and stories recounted in the workshop, a good-natured atmosphere where workers and the boss were pals. Because the business had grown, my father hired a secretary Marie, who was devoted to him heart and soul. She would prove it through the series of events that were already brewing. In my innocence at the time, I could not understand their scope or importance. After his operation, my father went to recuperate at the home of the family of one of his workers near Verdun. He took me with him and I discovered the joys of fishing and the simple life of country folk with the traditional Sunday pie and a passion for soccer. Wewent out to the soccer field in the afternoons as worthy fans of the men of that family who were all members of the soccer team. Thus I wound up spending my childhood in a Catholic milieu and far from my mother who still spoke to me in Yiddish. I might have been unaware that I was Jewish: my father was so assimilated that we did not even celebrate the Jewish holidays. At first, my mother tried to light candles every Friday night, but my father talked her out of it, because at the time they lived in a hotel room and my father asserted that the manager would throw us out for fear that they might start a fire. 1938. My parents decided to return to Poland for the first time to see their respective families. My mother's sister had arrived in Paris a few months earlier. My Aunt was pretty, brunette, thin, and educated. My mother on the other hand was illiterate because she had been obligated to work from a very young age. I was dazzled by this aunt who had so many stories to tell me and from whom I learned little by little about the family my mother had not told me much about. She had not done so because of a lack of time and her struggle to make a living. Even though our situation had improved, perhaps she was reserved and not comfortable wearing her heart on her sleeve. My mother lived in the shadow of my father, whom everyone admired. He was a good talker, charming, he knew how to read and write in French, and left all the women enraptured, myself included. In July 1938 I went to Triel-sur-mer near Dieppe with my aunt in charge of me. There was also the daughter of the concierge, Josette: a pretty young woman who also worked for my parents. My aunt, who was so happy in France and who had no intention of returning to Poland, convinced me not to accompany my parents to visit my grandparents, insisting that in Poland there were many huge flies, and thieves at every street corner. So I missed out on my only opportunity to know my grandparents and the rest of the family. It was during that visit that my paternal grandmother mademy father promise to respect the major Jewish holidays: Passover, Rosh Hashanah, and Yom Kippur. I can still see myself in the synagogue rue des Tournelles for those holidays. The men down below and the women up on the second floor; it struck me as unfair that we women were segregated upstairs. My mother was very serious and she read the prayer book the whole day long. On the other hand I saw a number of women spend the time gabbing amongst themselves. At the time I was not much of a believer; I was interested mostly out of curiosity and I considered the whole thing to be spectacle. The holiday I liked best was Passover for the simple reason that on that day the food was delicious: I loved matzoh ball soup, gefilte fish, hard-boiled eggs with salt water and at the end a mixture of apples and crushed nuts. 1939. People began to talk about a possible war with Germany. On the radio we heard Hitler vociferate, and I wondered at the time how a whole people could applaud those speeches, unless they were a populationof madmen. How did all those things happen? How can one people destroy another? One is almost forced to conclude that the German people contain in them a streak of peerless cruelty because of their Teutonic heritage. It was good form during that period to read Mein Kampf in order to be able to discuss Hitler's theories. I remember that it was a small red book with black lettering and that it struck me as a bad omen. Nobody in France at that time believed that war was coming; no one wanted to believe it. The war of 1914-18 had left so many wounds, so much fear, so many injured, and we were now among civilized people. And that is why our governments, in part out of cowardice, but also out of hope that the worst could be avoided, used appeasement. In fact they only strengthened the power over his people of that madman who thought he was G-d but who embodied the devil astonishingly well. War broke out in September 1939, and I was surprised as anyone when I noticed that my mother was pregnant. I felt at the time that grown-ups were perfectly illogical and Iasked for an explanation from my parents. Even at that time, I thought that people decided whether or not to have a baby and I didn't imagine that an accident could happen. I only remember that my mother in self-justification pointed out that it wasn't a bad thing, because now my father wouldn't be sent off to war. That shows how little she understood him, but in any event he had no military obligation because he was a foreigner. He was one of the first, despite my mother's tears, to sign up for the foreign legion. But I remember as if it were yesterday that on a very cold night with snow cracking beneath our feet, my father and I on our way home from the hospital where I had just discovered what a newborn is - my little sister. As it happened I was extremely surprised: she looked like a doll, and, most extraordinary, she had red fingernails as though she had had a manicure. My father chose her first name: Françoise, after, I believe, her maternal grandmother, "Frideley," and let me choose her middle name. I pickedViviane for my favorite actress at the time, Viviane Romance. Things happened very quickly around then. My father, fearing that Paris would be bombed, sent us off to the center of France, specifically to "La Chatre" in provincial France, to the home of his secretary's father. We were not welcomed warmly; in fact he refused categorically to take us in. The reason was that he did not see why his own daughter had not come with us, if the danger was so great. Our trip had been a hard one, besides. There were people crowded together everywhere in the train compartments and corridors, and to go to the bathroom was an expedition in itself: unknown arms lifted me off the ground and I was passed from arm to arm. At the time, I was ten years old, but I remember becoming friendly with a soldier, and for many months afterwards I continued to think about him. Thus, given that the father refused to take us in, we — my mother, my aunt, my sister, and me — descended upon city hall, as did all refugees at that time. The social worker, after listening to our sorry story, gave us an official form entitling us to stay in the man's house. Fortified by our legal right we re-descended upon his house. Needless to say, he greeted us with less than no enthusiasm, saying: "Fine, you have my daughter's room allotted to you, but I do not have to tolerate you in the rest of my house. You will therefore do me the courtesy of remaining in that room. As far as cooking goes, that is not my problem." We were so afraid that he would not even allow us in the house that we were relieved... So we bought a gas camping stove that we placed in the bathroom. After all the emotional upheaval we were happy. We had somewhere to sleep and eat. Because the room had been a young girl's bedroom, it was decorated with good taste. Little by little I tried to tame that old bear. I didn't find it difficult. Because I was a very good listener, he began to recount his life for me, and little by little we became friends. Later he invited us to dinner several times. In fact we were beginning to find life to be good when one fine day the house began to shake. My aunt, who didn't understand what was happening, had gone to a corner of the room with my sister Françoise in her arms and a cushion on their heads. Quickly, I realized that we were being bombed. I had learned at school that one must not under any circumstances remain in the house in such a situation. I therefore took charge and I led them out into the street where everyone was moving in the direction of the fruit seller's. I think that at that time they had requisitioned the wine cellars as shelters. To reach it we had to go across an open square. The planes flew above the square and strafed it. My aunt wanted to follow her exploit with the cushion by crossing the square right in the middle. I brought her to her senses, explaining, as I had learned at school that one must always go along the walls. We were lucky, because just at that moment a burst of machine-gun fire swept across the square. For the secondtime, I had perhaps saved the lives of my aunt and my sister. My mother, recognizing my good sense, always asked my opinion after that. When we arrived at the wine cellar, where already several families had congregated, we were dazed. How was it possible that planes had come to bombard such a small town? We later learned that a rearguard regiment had in fact taken refuge there, which explained the bombardment by the Italians who wanted to help their allies win the war. We remained hidden in that cellar for three days and three nights. Luckily for us, just above our heads was food. Thus with fruit, camembert, and a liter of orange juice, we resigned ourselves to our fate. We slept on fruit crates with blankets we had brought with us. In my childish mind, I said to myself: "one can't find a more tranquil town" and insisted that we had traveled three days and three nights to finally arrive in this paradise. After the scare was over we returned to our soft nest. The old bear, needless to say, refused to leave his house. Several days later my father arrived in military uniform. He had not had the chance to fire a single shot, for the very good reason that his cartridges were not of the same caliber as his rifle! O marvelous France who had such faith in the Maginot line that it refused to modernize its weaponry. I became more and more skeptical about the good sense of adults. Needless to say, my father received a cool welcome. My mother demanded to know why he had sent us off to this god-forsaken place, especially since a few days after our departure Paris was declared an "open city". Refugees were strafed on the roads; many died and were mourned by their families. Because of this situation a decision was made which could have been made earlier, but the suffering of the population mattered little to the government. All that mattered to them was that they were safe at the right time. Thus after the defeat, which happened a few days later, we made our way back to our homes.

# 3 The nightmare begins

It was the beginning of school in the fall. The French went on endlessly in praise of their victorious aggressor, those dear Germans who were so reasonable, so good to us, accepting that half of France would remain a free zone. We wound up believing that all was for the best in this best of all possible worlds. Even that it was beneficial for the French to be in the firm hand of the Germans. There was no lack of collaborators. The French militia was quickly put in place to help the Germans in their task. I think that the Germans themselves were amazed at so much collaboration. Even we Jews, who had heard the rumors circulating about the denunciations and pogroms against the Jews in Germany. We were persuaded that in France they wouldn't dare to do anything to us. France was in fact divided into two parts. One part was happy about the victory of the Germans and rubbed their hands together gleefully at the thought of the great business deals they could now make. The other part had memories of the previous war; they found our defeat to be a bitter pill to swallow and were inconsolable. I must admit that the greatest resistance was found among the working class. The railway workers in particular played a sizable role in making the German machine grind to a halt. General Giraud and later General de Gaulle gave hope back to the ordinary people. It is among such folk that one finds the majority of those who did their best to help some Jews escape from the diabolical plot to exterminate an entire people. If I am able today to write these lines, it is because that secretary, who's appropriate first name was "Marie", saved my father (no doubt out of loyalty) and helped us as well. But let us return to 1941 and the first decree against the Jews.

All foreign men of Jewish origin were ordered to go to the police station in their neighborhood, a "simple formality" they said, to conduct a census. Actually that was the second decree. The first was that every person of Jewish origin (even if only one of their grandparents was a Jew) had to make a declaration. We were all given a yellow star which we were obligated to wear at all times outside the home. Thus that morning my father and my mother went to the police station in the 12th arrondissement. Before entering the building they ran into a friend who was in tears. She told them: "Albert went into the police station and hasn't come out." Hearing this, my mother begged my father not to go in, but my father, perhaps out of pride, couldn't shrink back. He thus went in and didn't come out. Someone came to get me at school so that I might see him one last time. Thus all foreign men of Jewish origin were sent to so-called shelter camps and we had the right to visit, on Sundays as it happened. For us a new phase in our lives began. A commissioner for the Jewish question was named. Jewish businesses were confiscated. One fine day a commissioner came to affix seals on the doors of my parents' workshop. My mother found herself out of the business and they allowed her only one sewing machine. But they underestimated my mother, a valiant little soldier. She broke open the seals with the help of her friends and moved out a significant part of the merchandise. When a collaborator wanted to take over the business he realized that some of the merchandise was missing, and came for an inspection at our apartment. He didn't find anything, the merchandise was hidden on the third floor in the building. My mother had her own form of logic. Who would think that she had had the audacity to steal from her own workshop, and she was right. We lived right above it and it was thus easy during the night to move everything. The neighbor was a Jewish woman, the one above us as well, and the non-Jew who wanted to eat the Germans alive helped us as well. What a great opportunity to fool the collaborator who took our business. My mother thus regularly visited my father at the camp in Beaune-La Rolande which was guarded by French policemen. There were seven prisoners in each barrack. The inmates chose one of their numbers to be the leader. My father, of course, was one of the leaders, having accepted the position only because he thought he could thereby help his fellow Jews. Because of his polished French he easily impressed the native French guards. They put on plays, art exhibitions: they set up a real cultural life. In some sense they had the feeling that they were in summer camp. They even received permission to go into town when their spouses came to visit. Business was good for the local shopkeepers, but the Germans had gotten wind of the good treatment these Jews received. There was talk of transferring them to camps in Germany. My mother with her good sense always urged my father to run away. My father retorted that he couldn't do that, because he was the leader of his barrack; if he did, the entire group would be punished. My mother gave him an ultimatum: either resign from his leadership post or she would no longer come to visit him. He would be reduced to the soup they fed him at the camp; she would no longer send him loving little packages full of delicious things. He obeyed my mother's wishes. He resigned his position. The following weekend Marie came to get him, and he found refuge staying with her, with the consent of my mother. It was the only safe place my father could hide. Two weeks later the entire camp was transferred to Auschwitz and three of my father's best friends were among the deportees. Robert, who once during a leave went home, but his wife cried so much, lamenting that she could do nothing for him because she didn't have any place to hide him and that his presence put her and their daughter in danger so he went back to the camp and never came back. Albert who, like my father, had signed up to fight for France, but whom France disowned, never returned. Those in their naivety who did not believe anything bad could happen to them? Those who were not willing to do absolutely anything to save their own lives? One had to admit that the German death machine was perfect. Their genius for destruction had made provisions for every eventuality. The Germans used their victims to destroy other victims; that is to say that certain people were willing to do absolutely anything, and that word does not begin to convey the reality. Even those who served as Kapos in the concentration camps aided in the destruction of their own people, in a sense. I have often asked myself whether the survivors of that hell could ever forget, and if so, how they could lead a normal life? I think that in all cases the horror they were subjected to was inscribed forever in their genes, and that from generation to generation that anguish has been handed down, leading to many mentally ill today. Four years have passed since I began to write the first lines of this text. My life has changed a great deal, or rather much has happened. Some of these things belonged to my dreams and have come true, as often reality outstrips fiction. Thus today I enter my 63rd year with the same passion for people and things, a need for others, but I also remain open to others. What's wrong with our society is that people don't listen to each other. The result is that cry of despair which takes the form of divorce and of general indifference for one another. The rupture of families, the presence of television and video games has killed family relationships. People live together but don't really know each other. It is so much easier to leave one another because we are tied to no one. On the horizon we can once again see the hatred for our neighbors. Everything is open to reappraisal. The end of Communism in the Eastern European countries shook up the rest of the world, for no one really expected it. Everyone had accepted that the world was divided into two parts. Free men lived in democracies and the others lived under the yoke of Communist dictatorship, and now everything was open to reappraisal. In what direction would the Communist bloc go? Was Nazism rising up again on the horizon? Some maintain that the Holocaust never happened, that Jews invented it in order to better take power.

That theory is professed in legal tribunals throughout the world, in universities. Obviously it gives rise to some rebuttals, but not many. I find that when journalists report the facts, they bring to it a certain knowledge. If one can accept the fact that more than six million human beings were destroyed simply because they were Jews that would be convenient for those who are ready to once again take power and subjugate the world. "The time of assassins has come once again", a time when victims will be guilty of everything and yet of nothing at all. Let's return to the period when my father, having escaped from the Beaune La Rolande camp, found himself at his friend Marie's home. I only learned these facts later. At the time, in order to better protect my father, my mother told me that my father had disappeared. My mother was very discreet when it came to him. My mother and her sister Guenia essentially lived together. I must say more about my aunt Guenia, who played a very important role in our family life, in fact, more simply, in our lives. When she arrived in France in 1937 or 1938 with a tourist visa, she began to work in my parents' workshop. They made shirts and long underwear for men. Business improved, and my father gave my mother an astrakhan coat that he ordered from the furrier who lived off the stairwell across the way. I can still see his windows on the first floor across the courtyard, windows that remained lit until far into the night, for the very good reason that, because he worked alone, he had to work twice as long to satisfy his customers. Looking back on it, I think that the reason why my father ordered a coat from him for my mother, and then another for my aunt Guenia, that he was hoping that by getting to know my aunt, the situation might lead to a marriage between them. I think that either that committed bachelor was not ready for holy matrimony or my aunt, after going out with him one time, wasn't particularly interested in him. The fact remains that she got her fur coat, but because she did not have the money necessary to obtain an immigrant visa (through certain channels one could obtain papers), she soon found herself in difficult straits. I think that it was my mother's cousin who lived in the 18th arrondissement who introduced my aunt Guenia to Albert. One beautiful Sunday the entire family went to visit Albert and his family who seemed very fine to me at the time, but definitely from a different world than our own. It was there that my aunt Guenia was introduced to Albert, who was very nice but really not my aunt's type. He was captivated by her beauty and immediately fell in love. The only advantage that he had in my aunt's eyes was the fact the he was a French citizen, and that if she married him, she too would become French. On the other hand, it meant the collapse of all her dreams, for there was nothing of Prince Charming about him and furthermore, in terms of a job, he did the pressing in the tailor's shop and his salary did not allow for high hopes. If your papers weren't in order, the French authorities didn't hesitate to deport you. So pressured by events in these troubled times, aunt Guenia accepted to marry him and this decision influenced all of our lives enormously. My parents had found a studio apartment on the rue St. Nicholas, which they had repainted. I remember my aunt's tears and despair at that time at having to marry a man whom she did not, and never would, love. I can say that from the first day Albert was so devoted to her that he accepted everything she did and G-d knows the situation later became tangled. Up until the last minute she was prepared to break off her engagement. My parents persuaded her to not do any such thing, and that, after all, once married and having French citizenship; she could always refuse to live with him. That's what she decided to do at first. And I was silent; I tried not to be noticed and attempted to understand the situation. Therefore I was completely surprised after the wedding to see my aunt move to the rue St. Nicholas with poor Albert. My parents were both surprised as well. Some time later, they moved to the rue de Bercy in a two bedroom apartment that looked over the courtyard and that, compared to the apartment on rue St. Nicholas, appeared luxurious to me. My aunt Guenia had a nervous temperament and extremely vivacious, and Albert was very calm, a little dull, and not sufficiently energetic and ambitious, which exasperated my aunt. Albert constantly asked her, "Why do you get so worked up?" He was a music lover, with his ear always pressed up against the radio and after a while he no longer listened to the complaints of my aunt. In fact he enjoyed life, and demanded little. The person who really reigned over this world of women was my father. He decided what was good for them, and in this case what was best was that Albert and Guenia go to the markets and sell the shirts that he manufactured. But it was a disaster and I vaguely remember a story of rain and a storm that left the shirts lying in the gutter, because Albert was not fast enough to put away the merchandise. Therefore my father decided that it was for the best after all to let Albert press the suits and for my aunt to return to work in the workshop. After the birth of Françoise, my mother was too busy making shirts and boxer shorts and in any case didn't really care to occupy herself with a baby, so my parents hired a nurse who stayed several months and left us because of events. I still remember her petulance, her love of life, her taste for things done well. The cooking was excellent, the house impeccable, and Françoise, with her bibs always starched, always well groomed with a little bow in her hair, looked just like a little doll. Albert left for the war in the first months and was made a prisoner almost immediately. But the incredible thing was, he spent the entire war as a prisoner of war and a German officer developed a fondness for him and protected him against reprisals that would follow from his status as a "Jew." This officer was also a music lover: they had something in common, despite their difference in race!!! Therefore my aunt, once again single, shared her life more and more with us. That's the reason why, when my father sent us during the exodus to la Chatre, my aunt went with us, and it was she who provided us with food and took care of Françoise. I think that my mother immediately found sewing work at the corner grocer's, who was enriched by the war. Therefore between my mother, who was appreciated everywhere for her sewing work "always using a machine," and my aunt, who was always very talkative and who always found friendships easily, life appeared simple to me, especially since when my father wasn't there, we didn't have to suffer his authority. I don't have much recollection of a close relationship with my mother during this period, but my aunt took her place very well and she took me for a confidante, criticizing the indifference of my mother and the situation of my father staying in Paris with Marie and leaving us in this dump. So even if I was, at that time, a bit naïve, my aunt took charge of opening my eyes. When they spoke of my father, whether it was my mother or my aunt, they always called him "mister." They never used his first name. Maybe due to the fact that he reigned as master over his workshop of women and was the only man, he was easier to distinguish that way. To return to the time when my father escaped from the concentration camp, it was understood that he would take refuge at his secretary Marie's apartment, who had established only one condition: that my mother not ever visit my father, because this would be too dangerous.

My aunt scorned this arrangement, saying that it was obviously very convenient and that they could just enjoy their perfect relation. I did not see things the same way, and I thought at the time that we were very lucky to have a Marie.

# 4  Escaping the july 1942 Roundup

1942- Things moved more and more quickly. We heard that Jewish women and children were going to be rounded up. My aunt, who went with Françoise every afternoon to the square situated between Fauburg St. Antoine and rue Abel not too far from the Place d'Aligre, was sitting on a bench when she heard a policeman telling the women who were there with their children, "Don't sleep at your home tonight if you are Jewish. Tomorrow morning there is going to be a big round-up." This was the big round-up of the Vel d'hiv where thousands of women and children were packed together. At seven o'clock in the morning in the sleeping city the French police gave in and became accomplices to this felony: to arrest women and children who had done nothing, simply because they were born "Jews." Luckily, among them there were nevertheless men with consciences who did not accept taking part in this crime. This event occurred I think during the first two weeks of July. I remember I was already on vacation. The only thing that I remember is that my aunt came back home with Françoise in her arms and told my mother, "We cannot sleep here tonight, there is going to be a round-up tomorrow morning" and my mother responded, "But where can we go?" My aunt told her, "Come to my apartment. I got information from the police; I asked whether French women whose husbands are prisoners of war were included?" And the policeman replied "No, I don't think so, but in any event, if someone knocks, do not open the door and above all do not make any noise." My mother's mind was half made up. My aunt went to see my father at Marie's to inform him of the situation, and she returned with an order, "All of you go sleep at Aunt Guenia's." The net was tightening, and I finally realized that our life was in danger, In my innocence, I had not realized that this could happen to me and I still remember being in the middle of my second year at the school on the rue de Charenton, when one day in the courtyard a girl, following a little argument between us, told me, "I am more French than you." Outraged, I slapped her in the face and asked her, "What are you insinuating? Is it because I'm Jewish that you say that?" And she, embarrassed, responded, "No, I didn't mean that." And everyone in my class who had been present at the altercation went to report the incident to Mrs. Patrie, who was our schoolmistress. She made me come to her desk and said in front of the whole class, "Don't be ashamed of who you are. I can assure you that I would have been proud to have you as a daughter." That day I felt like a heroine from a novel and I became, it's true, the idol of the class: the righter of wrongs. Whenever some injustice occurred in class, the girls would come to me and ask for my help. Once, during a test, the best student in the class cheated, and as she was the teacher's pet, the girls were appalled. Therefore they came to me for a solution. So in the middle of the test I stood up and I said that someone was cheating. The schoolmistress, of course, asked me to name the girl. I refused, and in the end, the guilty girl gave herself up. Justice was served. I had two friends in that class: Colette C., who was an observant Catholic, and lived in a high-class building on the corner of rue de Crozatier and

21

avenue Dommesnil. I often walked with her, which allowed us to stay together longer. Sometimes we stopped at the square where I knew I'd find my aunt and little sister. My aunt always had bread and chocolate to offer us, from the black market obviously. All of the corner grocers knew her and she obtained everything that she wanted. The only thing that she needed was money and my mother, with her fingers like those of a fairy, took care of that, because at the time she redid collars and cuffs, taking the fabric needed from the bottom of the backs of the shirts. My aunt brought her clients. At around the same time, again using my aunt's contacts, my mother bought gold bars, which later permitted us to escape to the Free Zone, my father and the rest of us: Françoise, my aunt and me. So it was very fortunate that my mother, a veritable worker ant, amassed a little nest egg. My second friend, Jacqueline B., had suffered the deportation of her parents, and escaped the round-up thanks to her two brothers. I never saw her parents again. Jacqueline, who was a cheerful girl who was always laughing, never got over the deportation of her parents. She married later but I learned that she never wanted to have a child, for fear of another holocaust. I had the opportunity, some years later, to talk to her on the telephone. I wanted to see her, but she evaded the invitation. I think that she was broken forever. Maybe the same thing would have happened to me if I had lost my parents to deportation. The most terrible thing is that you never knew how they perished. You can only imagine, from what we know from witnesses, what had been their suffering, their physical degeneration, their despair. Therefore we went to my aunt's place in late evening and we took great care not to make any noise that might to wake her neighbors. Her neighbor on the same floor was Jewish and had three children. My aunt warned her to not sleep at her place, but unfortunately she didn't have any place to go. My aunt didn't explain to her that we were there for reasons of security. So there we were in the bedroom, with closed shutters and mattresses on the ground for my aunt and me, with my mother and sister in the bed, and we began our wait. Today, at the mere thought of it, my heart begins to beat wildly again, as it did that morning, when the sound of violent knocking on the door across from our apartment suddenly woke me up, followed by terrible screams and sobbing. The neighbor went to the window, calling for help and screaming threats if the policemen forced open her door: she would throw herself out the window with her three children. Alarmed by such determination and surprised by this attitude that didn't fit in with the stereotype of docility that we poor Jews had shown in the face of these assassins, they told her, "Calm down, we will come back later." Her courage saved her own life and the lives of her children. An ordinary woman, without an extraordinary personality, she was sublime. When the police came back she had found shelter at a neighbor's place, who had been moved by her courage. As for us, the hours began to weigh heavily. We remained in the silence that returned abruptly when the police left, as if nothing had happened. We heard some birds singing, happy to be alive and indifferent to human problems. My aunt, fearless, went out to get news. Very quickly we organized ourselves against the adversary; we had to construct a plan in order to try to save our lives, with, as it happens, all these women, all entirely devoted to my father, but also my mother, who had always protected them from my father. When shirt collars weren't sewn on correctly, in secret my mother undid them and redid them at top speed, because there was no one faster on the sewing machine. I think that machine was the love of her life second only to my father.

# 5 Escape to the Free Zone

. While the majority of Jews sought refuge in the Lyonnais region in the Free Zone, which in fact was under the control of the Germans, my parents, through some miraculous good fortune, decided to try to cross into the Free Zone and to go to the southwest of France, to a small village called "Lafox," 8 km from Agen, for the good reason that my mother had a cousin there. She, along with her husband and her two children, had taken refuge there at the time of the French defeat and had rented a farm there, a farm of about 100 acres. They had a herd of ten cows. They grew wheat, corn, and other crops that I don't recall. Marie and Jeanne found a smuggler for my father and my mother. In fact, it was train conductors who agreed to take people into the Free Zone who had good reasons for needing to escape from the Occupied Zone. I tip my hat to the railway workers and train conductors, who, before anyone else, tried to jam the German machine. So my father and then my mother crossed into the Free Zone in a locomotive and for them it was a relatively easy passage, provided you were not caught. As for my sister and me, it was urgent that we find another shelter than my aunt's apartment. My sister, Françoise, was a very well-behaved child who never cried, wasn't capricious, and who helped us a lot in our escapes. So we left for the North to stay with Jeanne's family, and she accompanied us as well. This worked well, because it was just at the moment of our school vacation. She passed us off as little cousins from Paris, who, the poor children, needed clean air and better food than that found in Paris. In the beginning, everything went very well. It was understood that we would go to mass every Sunday as well as to vespers, so as not to attract the village's attention. I went to the farm across the field, to get milk. There was a young couple: Jeanne's

sister and her fiancé, the two of whom were always kissing in every hidden spot they could find. I sang all of Charles Trenet's songs for them: "The Sun Has a Rendezvous with the Moon," "I'm Singing," "It's Raining in my Room." I was once again the star. At eleven and a half my body was changing and I was becoming a young woman. I made a friend in the village and unfortunately one day I thought I was doing the right thing to take her in my confidence and tell her the truth "that I was Jewish and that I had come to their village in order to hide." She swore that she would keep my secret, but 24 hours later the entire village knew and we had to move quickly. I was devastated by the consequences of my talkativeness. I, who had been the star, became an undesirable for this family that I put in danger. Obviously everybody in the family compared me, a girl of almost twelve, stupid and with a loose tongue, to my little sister of two and a half, who, either silent or gurgling, didn't create any problems for anyone. My stardom took a royal blow. After we returned to Paris, my aunt found a smuggler who led us into the Vierzon forest, left us there and promised us that at night a small boat would take us across into the

Free Zone. The smuggler left with the equivalent, at the time, of 500 francs. There were German soldiers in the forest who patrolled with German Shepherd's to prevent the possibility of escape into the Free Zone by escaped prisoners of war. I remember that I found myself nose-to-nose with a German soldier with his dog, who asked what I was doing there. I explained to him that we had come to spend the day in the forest, my aunt (supposedly my mother), my sister, and I, and seeing that my sister and me were blond and blue eyes, he left. Cheeks burning and body shaking it was miracle he did not see this and the dog was friendly to me, because I knew that my life might have been on the line, I went back to my aunt. Night had fallen much earlier, my little sister was tired and my aunt irritated, and we approached the bank where we were supposed to meet the boat at around ten at night, but nothing was on the horizon. We thought that the smuggler had tricked us and that nobody would come for us. After an hour of waiting, of constantly seeing the Germans' lights sweeping the river, a small boat docked. The smuggler had lost an oar, which had made him late, but when he saw us, he first refused to take us, insisting that he had been told that it was for an escaped prisoner of war. My aunt began to beg him to take us, explaining that her husband was a prisoner of war and that she had to escape the Germans; I began to cry. Finally out of pity he took us; he didn't have the heart to leave us there. He took us to the other side of the river, but we had to go 30 kilometers the next day, because if the French police caught us they would send us back to the Occupied Zone (that was a part of the agreement between Vichy and the Germans). He took us to his mother's to whom he introduced us as the wife of a prisoner with two children. My aunt had explained to my little sister that it was necessary to call her "Mom," and Françoise obeyed her orders to the letter. I, on the other hand, asking her for toilet paper to wipe my little sister, forgetting the orders, called her "aunt." Obviously our secret was out. The mother demanded an explanation from my aunt, forcing her to invent a story, that my mother had died and that she was replacing her and that it was for this reason that sometimes I made mistakes. Needless to say, when we were in the bedroom she called me all kinds of names, which was really pointless because I felt so guilty and thought myself extremely stupid. I was living a real nightmare, fearing each minute that I would forget my orders. The next day we left behind the previous night's rescuers. They hugged us all tenderly, advising us to walk thirty kilometers before taking the train. Marie had given me new shoes before my departure and like all respectable shoes; they were not really made for walking for such a long distance. The shoes were sheer torture. I couldn't stand it any more, and my aunt scolded me as we walked, saying that she couldn't understand how a big girl like me could be so stupid as to put on new shoes for travelling. This word "idiot," I heard it for years, and I ended up believing that I was really just that, which seriously undermined my self-confidence. The only way to be forgiven was to suffer in silence, but unable to stand it any more, I took off my shoes and finished the journey barefoot, like a gypsy.

It goes without saying that we ran into a policeman who, finding us a rather bizarre trio, stopped us and asked where we were going. My aunt invented a story that could put anyone to sleep and managed to confuse him by asking for directions to the nearest train station. I think we were very lucky to have run into a nice guy who advised us to take the roads across the countryside in order to avoid unpleasant encounters.

# 6 Our new life in Lot-et-Garonne

. I don't remember our journey itself; the only thing I recall is that we arrived in the town of Lafox about ten kilometers from Agen. It was a large farm owned by one of my mother's cousins who had come from Belgium with her husband and her two children. It was here that my parents had fled to. The cousin and her family had come in an old Renault which had since then taken up residence in a barn near a haystack. Thus at the beginning I was extremely happy to be reunited with my parents and cousins. I thought we had found some safety from the dangers around us and an easy life for me, but I didn't foresee what my father would do. To show our gratitude to the family that took us in, he proposed that I take care of the cows, a herd of ten animals. Like all good city folks, I knew absolutely nothing about the mentality of a cow. They had a pasture on one side of which was a field of corn and on the other a vineyard. The farmers had given them a mutt who was afraid of the cows, which meant that I spent all of my time running after those stupid cows. When I came back in, I was completely exhausted, but that didn't protect me from having to help milk those cows. Because I wore rubber boots without any socks, after a few days I caught a cold. What a relief! My father helped with the farm work. And inevitably, like in all good families, after only a few days the familial harmony was no longer very cordial. The little cousins were horrible towards me; I was their little servant, I was in their home. Luckily my father didn't have much patience for the female cousin who never stopped talking. So before there was a complete falling out my father went off to look for a haven of peace, obviously in the near-by towns. Believing themselves to be for once and for all safe from their executioners, my parents led an agreeable life for a certain period of time. They bought their food from

the farmers, for this was the region in which pigs were fattened to make all kinds of ham, and where geese were fattened to make foie gras. The southwest of France is known for its food; one eats well there, the countryside is beautiful, and for my father, who was a farmer then, it was wonderful because they also grew tobacco. Like usual, my mother came to my father's rescue: she sewed for the farmers and in exchange we had pork, goose, and tobacco. My mother was loved by the farm folk, because she did miracles with their old sheets, from which she created aprons and dish towels for the women, and shirts and underwear for the men. So, everything was going very well, but my father always had a gift for changing everything when he saw that everyone was happy. No longer able to bear the proximity of other refugees who mostly spent their time playing cards, and predicting that they would all be picked up one day because they stood out too much, my father managed to rent a house up in the hills, far away from all of those foolhardy compatriots, but by the same token far from everything else as well. The closest village was four kilometers away. Going there downhill was fine, but coming back up, one had to push one's bicycle or if one went by foot, one did well to stop from time to time to catch one's breath. Obviously we didn't often go to the village. The house was situated on a hillside that dominated the entire valley. You could see people approaching the house on the small road from at least a kilometer away. The closest neighbors were 500 meters lower down on the hill and on top of the plateau there were other farms. The farm belonging to the Dutch was the closest and above us, and a bit further down was the farm of the Vidals, who adopted us immediately. The house was charming and didn't look like a farm house at all. It was more like a villa that had been constructed by an artistic painter. It was in a slightly Provencal style with an entirely enclosed garden. On the side of the house was a barn. We were delighted to discover tomato plants in the garden. The garden was set out on a slight incline and at the end of it were an apricot tree, a fig tree, and a pine tree. Across the road from the house there was a small piece of land further up the hill, with three stone steps leading up to it. On that same side, there was a well of spring water on two levels. We got our water with a pail suspended at the end of a long pole, and water flowed gently down below into a pond for the animals. The house had a large stone chimney and a tiled kitchen was attached to the living room. The kitchen looked out on the back and side of the barn, with a door with small window panes looking out on the tomato plants. Within the living area was a bedroom with an alcove across from the chimney. Across from it were two steps that led to a large and lovely bedroom. And what a surprise! We discovered that the toilet was in the house. Normally at that time the toilet were at the far end of the garden in a wooden shack. It goes without saying that, once we discovered the charms of this house, all of our feelings of resentment against my father evaporated. My mother forgot all about her rich farmers down in the valley. Tobacco was grown at those lower altitudes and brought in more money than other crops. As my mother did not know how to ride a bike, she wouldn't be going down into town. My aunt, who loved to converse with the baker and the grocer, where she would learn about everything that was going on, felt completely trapped. This was the end of

September 1942, and my little sister Françoise was the only one not complaining. As for me, I had finished the last year of middle school, and I wanted to return to it. We had to get used to the situation. So, my father and I left for the village of Grand-Fond which was tied to this village. My father met the mayor who belonged to the Croix-de-Feux, which was a sort of French fascist organization, but he rather liked my father because he had set himself up on his own outside of the village and because he asked him for advice concerning buying a cow for milking and raising pigs, chicken, rabbits, etc. On his advice, my father enrolled me in the village school, so that I could obtain my "certificat d'étude" (basic diploma). It was also on the mayor's advice that my parents entered my little sister Françoise in a contest for the prettiest baby and she won. Suddenly we became well known. We got a cow that gave us 14 liters of milk a day and whom we called "Marquise". The pig was called "Roland" and he followed us around like a little dog. My father bought a dog that we nicknamed "Fifi" and life went on. Every morning I went off to school on my bike, and did part of the way on foot, because the hill was too steep. The school had two classes, one for the little kids and the other for the big ones (11-14 years old and even older); for farmers' kids came to school when they could, not during harvest time or when it was time to pick the grapes. Obviously, coming from the city, I was at a more advanced level than they, and the boys were mortified by my intellectual superiority. The teacher of the small kids, who was also the director of the school, liked me, and she loaned me books out of her personal library and asked me to help with her class when she had other things she had to do. At the beginning the boys tried to attack me physically. Luckily, when I tried to defend myself, I bloodied the nose of a boy who was the strongest. My reputation was made: I was the girl who hit back. Girls asked me to protect them. Obviously, most of the students ate at the school at lunchtime. We all took turns at the task of preparing beans, and the farmers brought lard for their kids. The upshot was that we were all very well nourished at that school. My teacher didn't much like me because I was from Paris. He ignored me the entire year, not wanting to help me pass the "certificat d'études". But the fact that I read a great deal helped me with grammar.

The big day finally arrived when five boys and one girl - me - went to take the test. We left by bicycle for the town of Puymirol which was also in the hills. Not surprisingly, the boys were better on a bicycle than I was. I couldn't manage the steep climbs. The teacher acted indifferently and made no effort to help me. Finally, unable to go any further, I stopped and began to cry. I thus did manage to move them and for the remainder of the journey they competed amongst themselves to be the one who helped me most. We made a triumphal entrance into town: I surrounded by my boys, numbering five. Next we underwent the sports test and once again they beat me hands down. I was in despair, and after the oral exam, I learned that their answers were completely different from my own, so I was sure that I had failed. What a surprise then for me when the results arrived and I was the only one who passed. The teacher was so mortified that he didn't even congratulate me. That was the end of a carefree period for me, yet again; more difficult times were in the offing. Having passed my tests, the only thing I was really thinking about was going to school in Agen where I would obviously be a boarder. I daydreamed about the good life of a student, doing nothing, living in a dormitory, having friends and a school uniform. I don't know whether my parents really intended to send me to a high school, but in any event circumstances made the decision and it was a different one. First, I realized that my mother was pregnant. I asked my parents what kind of idea it was to have another baby during that period, but rumors were afloat that there were to be new arrests, that men were going to be put in concentration camps, but that if one had three children, one might be exempt from the round-up. In any event my baby sister arrived on May 31, 1943. I don't remember whether my mother went to the hospital; I think she may have given birth in the house. For me it was the beginning of diaper duty. Needless to say I found it disgusting to clean poop; I can still see myself at the well, delicately holding the diaper between my hands and rinsing it for hours before I would consider really touching it. We lived with my aunt Guenia, and we had grown accustomed to having her do certain tasks that neither my mother nor I liked doing. She was also very adept at bring us provisions from the farmers. She was always afraid that we might lack something. The period brings to mind the time when we made "cottage cheese" out of milk. The cream from the top of the cottage cheese was scooped up and put into bottles and we spent hours shaking these bottles in order to make butter. Out of all the fruits and tomatoes my mother and my aunt made jam. I have never since encountered tomato jam, but at the time, I thought it marvelous. During this period my father made several attempts at planting, but without much success. The lands that we had were full of stones and nothing much would grow there. We planted three bags of potatoes. Worms got them and we harvested barely one bag. Next we tried peas. They were ready to harvest, but we waited one day too long. Rabbits got them. The pig weighed 70 kilos when my father bought it. We fed it constantly and after three months he had lost weight and was now hardly over 40 kilos. My father decided to kill it, with the help of some farmers. It seems that the pig had a tapeworm. That didn't stop us from eating it. It was astounding how many friends suddenly came to visit and enjoyed part of that pig! After a year our cow "Marquise" stopped producing milk. And it was my job to lead her out on the road to graze. At first some farmers had rented a pasture to us, but later they changed their mind and would no longer rent that pasture to us. That cow was super intelligent. When I wanted to bring her back home, she began to limp, but when she wanted to escape from me, she would take off running with no sign of a limp. Then there was the story of the dog, which one day brought us back a rabbit. We allowed her to eat it. She developed a taste for fresh meat, but found it much easier to do her hunting in our hen house, and began to kill the chickens that were meant for us. It goes without saying that my father was upset. He killed the dog and made me bury her in the small patch of land further up the hill from the house, but the story got more complicated. Not long before, Fifi had had six puppies. My father only kept one of them and commanded me to go drown the other five, for the farmers didn't want them, and it was on their advice that he told me to drown them. At the bottom of the hill there flowed a river, but in certain places one could ford it. I was traumatized, for this is not a job for a twelve-year-old child, and it was a time of war when people were killed in bombing raids and others were mercilessly executed for acts of resistance. Who, I ask you, was going to feel sorry for these little puppies? I did not have the heart to carry out the sentence. I delicately placed them on stones in the middle of the river, telling myself that perhaps some good soul would take them in. In the meantime we had become accustomed to killing rabbits, skinning them, killing and plucking chickens, but that was in no way comparable to burying a dog that you loved, that your father killed. And every night the son of that dead dog tried to dig her up, and every day I had to yet again do that nightmarish task of burying her, and little by little the dog was devoured by worms so that nothing was left but the skin. But why was it necessary that the dog be buried over and over so that no one would be able to see her? Simply because no one would believe that women could kill a dog. One day, the police knocked at the window of the bedroom that faced the road. They came to pick up my father again. After a new agreement between Vichy and the Gestapo, it was understood that foreign Jews were no longer protected in the Free Zone and would be handed over to the Gestapo. At first, this policy was limited to men. That reminds me of that day in July 1942 when we were hidden at my aunt's. The same knocks at my neighbor's door made my heart beat so wildly in my chest that I thought I was going to pass out. It was at that moment that I first prayed to G-d, asking him to save my father. But now, we had heard refugees saying something was up, so we were on the alert. Before we opened the shutters, my father escaped into the barn from the kitchen and hid in the hay. Obviously we hadn't opened up immediately. At the time, I hid my head under the sheets, so my aunt, who slept in the same room, opened the shutters. The police were surprised that we hadn't opened them more quickly, and seeing my feet sticking out beyond the sheet, asked who was under the covers. I got out of bed, knowing that my father had escaped. My aunt told them that my father had left several days earlier and that she didn't know where he was. The police left somewhat skeptical, and made inquiries with the neighbors. The Dutchman, with whom moreover we were on good terms, said that he had seen my father the day before. So the policemen came back and searched the house from top to bottom; then they went into the barn and stuck the pitchfork into the hay. Miraculously they did not find my father. Obviously, that marked the beginning of a new way of life for us and for my father. We all had to act as though he were not there. And it is clear that no one would have believed that two women and a girl of thirteen were capable of killing a dog, thus the fear that one of the neighbors might see the dog's carcass. From that moment on, my father began his life as a recluse, and we our lives of constant watchfulness, especially when my father listened to the forbidden BBC programs on his radio: "PAM PAM PAM PAM" barked the radio, saying "from London, Frenchmen speaking to Frenchmen." Of course that "Pam Pam..." was significant, and it was forbidden to listen to the British radio, under threat of arrest, but for us it meant hope, hope for the end of this nightmare, the defeat of the "Boches", liberation. Hope of becoming normal people again, of no longer being hounded like animals, of no longer being treated like undesirables, even though we were unaware at the time of what was really happening to the Jews. Those who were deported. The same radio station told us that there were rumors that those who were sent to Germany were crammed into cattle cars. But at the time, no one suspected the reality: crematoriums and gas chambers. It was only later, when the Allied troops liberated the death camps that the full horror of that reality came to light. Nothing can ever be wiped clean. Those crimes against humanity will for all eternity hang over the people who blindly followed that bloodthirsty madman, and who thereby destroyed the soul of that nation for ever. Even today after more than fifty years have passed, a German is always uncomfortable telling you his nationality. For me the German land is accursed: too much blood was shed, too many human lives were destroyed. Of course they were not all guilty for all of these atrocities, but the majority were guilty of accepting the situation. There was almost no resistance in Germany. They all, or almost all, believed in the superiority of the German race over all others. They felt no remorse, no compassion, for all the harm they did. They lost their souls. They dreamt only of revenge and supremacy. They learned nothing from their defeat. In some sense they degraded themselves to sub-human status. Listening to the radio was our only lifeline. Whenever we learned that the German troops had suffered a defeat on the Russian front, it was like a breath of fresh air. One day my father was listening to the radio and I was keeping watch on the hillside road, when suddenly I heard the sound of boots and before I was able to make a move, there appeared a battalion of Germans in front of the house. They came from the opposite hill. Not knowing what to do, not daring to move, but hearing the sound "Pam Pam Pam" and fearing that I would attract their attention if I took off into the house, I stayed glued to the spot. I remember that one or two of the soldiers waved to me and I waved back. Slowly I went back toward the house. Without a word, incapable of speaking, I turned off the radio, pointing to the window. My father then understood what was happening. We learned only later that this battalion had attacked the fort where resistance fighters were hidden. They were all killed. I think that the Germans were happy at their success destroying this commando unit of resistance fighters, and tired. It was our good fortune to escape massacre, or perhaps it was because I responded to their wave without even thinking that we were the beneficiaries of their benevolence. I remember another time when they were kind to me. We had a cherry tree, and I had the idea to take the cherries into Agen to try to sell them. My bicycle didn't have tires, but only rims, and a little cart was attached to the bicycle. There I was with 40 kilos of cherries in the cart setting off on an adventure like Perrette and her milk jug. A little before arriving in town, I had to cross some railroad tracks and, looking up, I saw a German soldier standing at attention in the front of the garrison. With a queasy feeling in my stomach that I always got whenever I saw a green uniform, I neglected to look where I was going. I wanted to get out of there as quickly as possible, but I took the bend too sharply, the cart got stuck between the tracks, and I was thrown to the ground. Two soldiers, who were nearby hurried to help me get up. I was scared to death and couldn't refuse their help. I didn't even clean off my wounds, wanting only to flee. They were not insistent, understanding no doubt that I was scared by their uniform and thus didn't want their help. Those wounds took a very long time to heal, and the family treated me like a heroine, especially since I sold those cherries and brought home 20 francs. Things moved quickly: there was the Normandy landing, the retreat of the Germans on all fronts, the liberation of Paris. I remember that when Agen was liberated I took my mother to the Agen cinema in the bicycle cart. On that day the air seemed to be lighter. I couldn't believe that we were free and alive.

# 7 Return to liberated Paris

Several days later my father and I set off for Paris. My mother planned to return to Paris, but a bit later when everything had calmed down, for there were places where the Germans were still fighting. Paris had just been liberated by the Resistance; the American army was not yet there. In Agen collaborators were being arrested. Some were shot. Women who slept with Germans had their heads shaved and were paraded through the city. Some collaborators changed sides at the last minute and became final-hour resistance fighters, which allowed them to stay safely within the system. At the time I found it highly unjust that these poor women who had done nothing but sell their bodies had to pay such a high price, while it was often collaborators who had many crimes on their conscience who focused the public anger on these poor women. whose only crime had been to better their daily life. We were only at the beginning of the purges which lasted only a short while.

Afterwards, the justice system took over and the trials began to drag on. My only joy was to learn of the deaths of Doriot and Laval who had done all they could to help the Germans destroy my people, guardians of the Torah, guardians of G-d's law. This people, who have never accepted submission, despite all the tortures they have had to endure, despite the destruction of the first temple, and four hundred years later of the second temple, slavery in Egypt, the Spanish Inquisition, despite all the persecutions, executions, pogroms, the Holocaust, and terrorism. After more than five thousand years this people is still faithful to their beliefs. They deserve the respect of other races. They do not try to convert others. The time has perhaps come for other races to acknowledge their learning, their spirituality, their soul, and for others to no longer blame them for all the ills of the earth. Those ills guide dictatorships, government and individual selfishness,

and the ambitions of certain people who imagine that power will give them invincibility from illness and death. The only power that we hold in our hands is to do good, to love one another, to forget about oneself. The more you give, the more you shall receive. I pity the person who has only hatred in his heart, for he destroys himself. Who are these people who are capable of torturing other human beings? To do so, they must first kill their own souls; their mental destruction precedes the destruction of others. An assassin destroys himself at the moment of committing his crime. Nothing can bring it back to life, even if society pardons him. He is dead at the moment of his crime. He killed the other, but also killed himself. So, as soon as we heard that Paris had been liberated, we hit the road. That must have been the last day of August 1944. I urged my father to go back to Paris because I hoped to return to the school on the rue de Charenton. My last school year had been the second middle level in 1942. Two years later, I wanted to go back to school; I had a thirst for learning. It took us six days to get to Paris for the train lines had been cut. We had to walk for hours to get to another train station while rail workers replaced the tracks. In certain places the Germans had blown up the tracks, and in others it was the Resistance fighters who had done so in order to hamper the German retreat. I was thirteen and a half, but looked eighteen, for the war and fear had made me mature quickly. I had lost my illusions about humanity, but I was very happy that I was alive and that those close to me had escaped the massacre. When we got to Paris I thought that my father and I would stay together, and I did not understand at the time why he brought me to the home of "the Aunt". We called her that because she had earned her status by virtue of her stature and her General-like character. No one argued about her orders: husband, children, or workers. It was for this same aunt that my mother began to work when she first arrived in Paris from Poland. Over the years, relations between my parents and this aunt had grown more distant. Intimidated by this woman, I really did not want to stay with her, but my father wouldn't budge, so I had to give in. All of my questions —where would he live? Who would take care of him?—were not answered. He had too much to do getting our belongings back, to be burdened taking care of a kid like me. We made a visit to the director of the Rue de Chareton School, for what was most important to me was getting back to school. Given my height and my maturity she placed me in the first year "cours complémentaire" (Junior High School), allowing me to skip the preparatory class. It goes without saying that even if I had obtained my certificate of study and an exemption, I was still a year too young. Having not been in class for an entire year, there were significant gaps in terms of my level of knowledge. She thought she was doing me a favor, but in fact it was the worst thing that she could have done to me, because I was unable to follow what was going on in class in several subjects and I ended the school year sickened and having lost confidence in myself. In the euphoric spirit of the days following the liberation of Paris, and with the help of the FFI, my father was able to get back his clothing workshop. He threw out the profiteer of the misfortune of others who had obtained our workshop with the aid of the minister of Jewish affairs. What a feeling to be back again in that place where my parents had worked so hard to obtain a little material well-being. What crime had my parents committed to deserve being stripped of their place of work and hunted as they were? As for the apartment, unfortunately after a short period of euphoria, one could no longer take justice into one's own hands with the aid of the FFI. Governmental administration was put in place and we had to wait two years to get our apartment back. Throughout this period I lived with that aunt I mentioned, who, to my great surprise, treated me with much tenderness. That woman spent her days crying, filled with remorse, for she had, in order to save her own life, sacrificed the life of her son David, that cousin I so deeply loved. She had three sons: Phillipe, the eldest, Joseph, and David. Philippe was with his wife in Limoges which was in the Free Zone. They had only one son. My great uncle and Joseph were deported and David remained with his mother. One morning several months before the liberation, David who always, for the sake of security, slept at a neighbor's place, heard his mother screaming for help. The French police, doing their last sweep, had come to arrest this woman who was so heavy she could hardly get around. David ran to her aid for she was yelling "David! David! Help me!" He managed to convince the police to take him in her place. Of course he never came back and she never forgave herself. At first I blamed her as well, for a mother's job is to sacrifice herself for her children, but later I realized that her remorse was literally eating her up. She fell ill because of it and died shortly thereafter. I also remember that shortly after our return to Paris my father took me to the Bois de Boulogne where the American army was stationed and that an American soldier gave me my first pair of stockings, some chewing gum, and some chocolate. That memory is as clear in my mind as if it were yesterday. What excitement! Those soldiers in their beige uniforms represented the free world for me. No longer having to look at those green uniforms or the SS in their black uniforms! What a relief! Sometimes I awoke suddenly in the middle of the night, wondering whether it was true that we were free, free to walk, to sing, to think, to cry, of no longer having to wear that Jewish star, as though it were a disgrace to be Jewish. At the same time the media was bringing us all those images of a horror we could not imagine. Sometimes I tried to envision myself in those death camps and a chill ran down my spine. Sometimes I felt guilty for having avoided the suffering inflicted on all the others who did not have my good fortune. Those skeletal bodies that were barely able to hold up their heads, whose faces reflected all the despair and horror of which they had been both witnesses and victims. Only once did my father bring me to Marie. It was a few days after we got back to Paris. I remember that at the time I was shocked to find one of my favorite books, David Copperfield, half torn up. My books were keeping Marie warm. I said nothing. What could I say to the woman who had saved my father's life, who had sold the merchandise that my mother had stolen, and risked her own life in so doing, and who had enabled us to survive.

I realized on that day that my father had a second life that I was unaware of. But what did it matter, for we were alive, and the sun rose for us once again full of hope and full of promise.

Many years later I learned from my aunt Guenia that Marie had died of a heart attack that she had never married, but had had two children, a boy and a girl.

# 8 My Teenage Years

. My father was in no great hurry to bring my mother, my two sisters, and my aunt back to Paris. I believe that after several weeks, my mother decided that enough was enough, and as was typical of important decisions, she just showed up without any warning. Everyone moved into the workshop as best we could. The two rear rooms served as our apartment and the two front rooms as store, workshop, and office. My parents found some of their old employees, most of who worked out of their own apartments, and my father was able to obtain a quota of merchandise, that is to say pieces of fabric from which he could make men's shirts and pajamas. While most manufacturers sold their merchandise on the black market, my father the hero began looking for his former clients and delivered to each a certain number of shirts and pajamas.

These very clients perhaps resold those items on the black market, and in any event when times got better they forgot all about this honest supplier. My mother who had common sense was naturally not in agreement with this system, because my father could have sold these items to new hungry customers desperate to get any merchandise, with a much higher level of profit. Thus while others made a fortune at all levels and were able to buy stores and apartments, we remained in our workshop/apartment waiting for the goodwill of the judges to give us back our apartment. But my father did not want to play the game and with our legally acquired points we didn't advance very much; after my year at school, my father decided that he needed me to help with running the business, so he enrolled me in the Pigier business school. Thus I went to the classes in the morning and in the afternoon I took care of the billing. It was nonetheless a good period for me. I had met a teenager, Paulette, who became my best friend for a while. I enjoyed looking at her because she was so pretty, like a model. She was tall, thin, dark haired, with big black eyes with long lashes, a perfect nose, and a beautiful mouth. Her smile showed off her perfect teeth. Everything about her bearing and her walk was harmonious. I became her best friend, her confidant. Through my contact with her, I became more attuned to beauty, clothes, and culture. She came from an old bourgeois family in which good manners were important. Her mother was separated from a man who held an important position in the government. She got divorced, for that man who was so charming in high society, was a cruel tyrant at home. That woman, whom I much admired, was still very beautiful. She always wore her hair up in a bun and, oddly enough, had a white streak in the front, which made her look even classier. So we took our Pigier classes together. They were the mold out of which came battalions of secretaries on the march for work. It is true that at the end of the year, you were educated, well or poorly. It depended on you and your abilities. There was no theory, only practice. Paulette was excellent at stenography and I drank in, like mother's milk, accounting classes. We had typewriters and I adored the Underwood. I loved the keys and the sound they made. Every day we finished at about 1 PM. Of course I was supposed to go home right away because the billing awaited me, but Paulette and I often took the long way home, often stopping at the Place de la Bastille, where often there were fairs, to have fun on the bumper cars. Then she went off in one direction, the Rue St. Antoine to St. Paul, where she lived with her mother and her brother in an old historical building from the eighteenth century, a three-room apartment that looked out on the courtyard and that was full of objects from a glorious past. I on the other hand, went in the opposite direction, the Faubourg St. Antoine neighborhood, the territory of furniture makers, most of who were well-established and had salesmen on the doorstep who called out to you. I hated their comments which were often in poor taste, and in order to avoid them, I walked very quickly and well out on the sidewalk. But I must admit that when I heard a young salesmen compliment me by saying "Oh she's cute!" or "What lovely legs" or "What beautiful eyes", it pleased me. All of this happened in 1946 when I was 15 years old. Life was good. Little by little I forgot the anxieties of wartime; the future was mine. I could dream about the Prince Charming who would come to free me from the tyranny of my father, who, when he was in a good mood, could be the world's best father. For vacation, he had rented a house in Sables d'Olonne in the Vendée region, but right then I had to work and work very hard, selling the collection of shirts to boutiques. It was difficult for me to even enter the boutiques because of my shyness. My friend Paulette, who had a boyfriend, told me about her arguments with him (he was very jealous), which she didn't like at all, because she had already been through the same thing with her parents. Her father was jealous which led to her departure. I think that her parents were not in fact divorced, and that her father's way of pressuring her mother was not to provide financial support. While we were at the Pigier School, Paulette found a job as a secretary in a prestigious company thanks to her lovely appearance and her dexterity as a stenographer-typist. I on the other hand played with numbers, and had to have a special dispensation to take the test for assistant accountant, because I was under sixteen. I was the only one of eighteen students who passed and the most surprised of us all. I can still see myself standing, completely dumbstruck, when the professor called out my name, because I was sure that I had failed the test. For me, the test results changed nothing. My destiny was to serve my father in any capacity needed, and that included filling orders, making packages, shipping, billing, secretarial work, errands, the bank, and the vacuum cleaner. Furthermore, I was not paid. I was made to understand that my parents were starting over again from zero and that money was tight, and that was true. With his moral principles, my father struggled with financial difficulties. What I hated most was when I was sent to see the banker to ask him for easier terms on the due date for monies owed at the end of the month. I understood even less, why whenever someone came to our house meanwhile, they mistook our house for that of the good Lord, and why not? They were fed, laundered, and housed. The true house of the Lord. Given that my father had someone who took care of all his paperwork, he could devote himself to his charitable works on behalf of former combatants. He displayed a whole array of medals he had received for I don't know what reasons. He loved medals, so every time there was a parade then, he went out to march with the veterans (he hadn't gotten off a single rifle shot; his rifle didn't work properly) or with the former deportees. And he had such a confident bearing and so much conviction that people really thought that he was important. My mother and I were both witness to all this play-acting. He loved to be honored. He would have done well in a government position, for he had no business sense and everyone knows that ministers waste the money that taxpayers worked so hard to earn. Thus, after going to see the banker who would help us make it to the end of the month, we were ready to go off on vacation, or rather, that year, my mother, my two sisters, and my friend Paulette went off to Sables d'Olonne, because I had to stay and help my father with all the shipping and billing for the fall, which would make life a little bit easier. Imagine my surprise when I finally made it to Sables d'Olonne: I didn't recognize my own mother. Paulette had completely transformed her. She, who had never really been interested in fashion, was dressed up, made up, laughing, and they were busy telling each other their secrets. I couldn't get over seeing the influence my friend had on my mother. I had the feeling that there was a bond between them that I had never myself had with my mother. That wasn't entirely true. I had a bond with my mother, but it manifested itself only in our shared opposition to my father's orders which neither of us ever followed to the letter. After that vacation I only saw Paulette again once or twice. I was very disappointed. Her mother invited me to lunch one day. I was very excited at the thought of seeing my friend again and could not understand why she wasn't present at lunch. That was the end of our friendship. I ran into her two years later in the metro; she was beautiful and sophisticated, and told me that she worked for a production company and that she might have a chance to be in a movie. That same year a crisis broke out between me and my father. I realized that I was being exploited and that I had no independence. Wanting to buy a dress for a special occasion, I had to ask my father for the money. He refused, saying I didn't need it. I went on strike and decided that I would find a job elsewhere and be paid like everyone else. Of course my father flew into a fury, but couldn't change my mind. I was ready to die for my cause. My mother couldn't make me see things his way and my father, for the first time, had to give in. It was decided that I would be officially salaried, but that a part of my pay check would go into a savings account in my name, an arrangement I accepted. From that day forward I no longer had ask for money every time I wanted to buy myself something. Life took on meaning for me. I developed self-confidence and I realized that I could say no. I also decided to go back to school, because I wasn't satisfied with what I was. I wanted to become at least an expert accountant. So I enrolled in the Paris Chamber of Commerce School on the Rue de Naples. I was accepted because of my assistant accountant diploma. I had to work very hard for there were certain gaps in some subjects in my education. Thus I sometimes worked until two or three in the morning. My father wasn't happy about the situation because he had to take on a part-time secretary. He found a solution to his problem. My parents went to Marseille in order to protest against the embargo on the exodus boats full of concentration camp survivors who wanted to go to Israel. I couldn't refuse: for two weeks I was in charge of the entire workshop, the clients, the billing, and my two sisters. At the time, gas was rationed; a friend had obtained gas coupons for us and I had to pay him. When my parents came back from their crusade, everything was in good order: the manufacturing process, shipping, and billing. My sisters looked well; I had taken good care of them, helping the elder, Françoise, with her homework, telling stories to the younger Annette. Everything went smoothly, but of course I had been sacrificed yet again, for I couldn't attend my classes. It was impossible to catch up in the Chamber of Commerce School, if one was two weeks behind. And my father, who can be beguiling at times, convinced me that it wasn't good for me to study half the night, and so I dropped out. Around that time my mother realized that I was lonely, that I didn't go out, that I spent all my free time reading. She habitually went to the Rue de la Forge Royale to buy a certain kind of Jewish pastry. In that pastry shop worked the daughter of the confectioner whose husband had been deported and who had two other daughters. Charlotte was my age, seventeen. She was the kind of person who just glowed with good health. She had very short, curly, blonde hair, a small nose, a mouth with braces, and pink cheeks. She really wasn't a complicated young woman. She smiled all the time. She had a very special smile. Her upper lip turned up on itself like a little cat. She really was a soothing person and we had a good time together. We both loved to dance. So every Saturday night, we went dancing. It was a good time, we didn't have many cares. I was seventeen. I was learning that I was perhaps more attractive than I had thought. I was quite popular. Around this time, one of my father's first cousins, Guedale, came to visit. He was the opposite of my father: always smiling not complicated, always in a good mood. He made me laugh until I cried. I liked him a lot, but that was all. I felt a good deal of friendship towards him, but he wasn't my type. I think he misunderstood my feelings. Perhaps my father had a little plan in the back of his mind. He sent us off to look for a little boy named Jeannot at a foster home. He was the family secret: my aunt Guenia had had this little boy during the Occupation as a result of a so-called passing infatuation. I finally understood why my aunt had disappeared right after the birth of my little sister Annette. In the train, Guedale tried to kiss me, and when I wouldn't let him, he said the following incredible thing: "Don't be childish." But he didn't keep trying and seemed to understand that I wasn't attracted to him, and because he was a smart guy, it had no effect on our friendship. Later I learned that he had had a child, Robbi, with a German woman who, I believe, wasn't Jewish, but he married her after she converted to Judaism. Robbi told me thirty years later that his father had been very much in love with me, but that I had rejected him. Of course, when Guedale and I saw the little boy we looked at each other because he was the spitting image of my father, and we no longer had any doubt about the paternity. My father had decided to live up to his obligations. This could have set off a major drama in our family, but to think that would be to not know my father. He was there to reestablish justice and his conscience told him to take care of this little boy, a task he imposed on my mother. His explanation was that Abraham had one wife but several concubines. So Jeannot was raised with my little sister Annette and they were playmates. In fact, several years later, Annette admitted to me that Jeannot was her favorite sibling. And my mother was sublime. In her opinion it wasn't the children's fault that adults behaved badly. My aunt's husband, Albert came back from Germany, one of the last prisoners. He had no objections to raising this son who had appeared out of the blue. My aunt had three other children, twin girls and a boy, and later on I realized that they all had the same father. Ironically, they all inherited my father's nose, like an indelible mark. It was more or less during the same period that I found myself one day walking on the street where my father's ex-secretary lived, and there was my father's car parked near her place and I suddenly understood that the relationship between her and my father was still going on. Several years later my aunt informed me that Marie had two children: a boy and a girl, and that she died of a heart attack. I understand today just how complicated my father's life was, and that in fact it is often thus. We three, his legitimate daughters, we never really knew him. His moodiness may have been due to his complicated life. Throughout, my magnificent mother let him get away with it all, with her philosophy that one can't be unhappy all one's life; one has to be happy some time. Today, I wonder: Did he realize what he was doing? But why have all those children? Perhaps in his own mind he was doing them a favor: without him they might never have had children. And also, he was able to fulfill his dream of having sons, as he hadn't had any with our mother. My mother often told me that I had the same temperament as my father, and that was why I could never get along with him. My father's friend Jacques who had returned from Auschwitz was really his best friend. We all went on vacation together. We were often invited to his place. He was an extremely kind man. He had suffered a great deal and that experience gave him a kind of indifference towards things. He had tried to take my father into business with him. Jacques had found some partners and they bought and sold fabric in bulk on the black market which, at the time, wasn't very legal. Jacques and his partners rapidly made a lot of money, but my father would have nothing to do with their business. He didn't much care for his friend's wife. They all went together to the dances to celebrate the end of the year.

# 9 The love of my life Maurice

. That year, in December of 1948, my destiny took shape. I had planned on going dancing with my friend Charlotte at, I believe, the Moulin Rouge in Montmartre where we liked to go. We had met two very amusing brothers and we decided to have a good time, but fate decided otherwise, or rather, my father decided that I would accompany them with their friends to the "Lotz" dance. Of course I refused, but on that particular occasion, my father dug in his heels. Thus, having no choice, I had to give in and go with them. It goes without saying that I went to that dance with considerable resentment. I was insistent that we not come home too late. From my point of view, only people who were interesting in eating went to that dance and I was going to be bored to death. For lack of better options I was dancing with Esther, Jacques's daughter, who was two years younger than I, when she said: "Look. That guy won't stop looking at you. Maybe he'll ask you to dance." I responded: "Normally when a guy looks at you, he never asks you to dance; it's just a game." In fact I thought he wasn't bad-looking, not at all. I couldn't understand why he had come to this dance with all these uninteresting people. After that dance, my father offered me a glass of wine. He now wanted to be forgiven. And suddenly he said: "I think someone wants to talk to you." I turned around and there was the good-looking stranger who asked me, as if in a dream: "Would you like to dance?" I couldn't believe my eyes or my ears. I, the little duck, was being asked to dance by this beautiful swan. It was the beginning of a beautiful love story, one that lasted 39 years, and that could only be ended by death, if by that. The memories have been preserved intact, the bond, the spirit, the happiness that we shared. The ups and the downs, the moments of pleasure, the sorrows, all that makes up a life. From the moment of our first meeting we were as one. For us the world no longer existed. He had a sense of humor that I found enchanting. He made me laugh until I cried. Even during our first dance, our feet moved together perfectly. I looked at him furtively, wondering whether he was Jewish, for with that perfect little nose, he didn't really look Jewish. I have always been a bit skeptical: when things are too wonderful I don't believe they're true. And this was too beautiful to be true. As it turned out, it was a complete accident that he happened to be there that night. A friend who was to meet a young woman at the dance had brought him along. After we danced, I went back to my parents and chatted with Esther. Suddenly I saw that my handsome stranger was dancing with a girl who looked ordinary with heavy makeup. I was so disappointed, above all else, by his bad taste: how could he ask that kind of girl to dance? Once again, I congratulated myself for not having gotten too carried awayAfter that dance ended, I was still lost in my thoughts when he came up to me to ask me to go up to the second floor with him, where there was another group having a dance, in this case the leather goods craftsmen. My first reaction was to send him away. But after a little reflection, I gave him the benefit of the doubt, especially given his explanation that his friend has asked him to dance with that girl while he went to see somebody. He said he was very unhappy to have to dance with her, but couldn't refuse the favor for his friend. After that we didn't leave each other's side the entire evening. I was in seventh heaven. I had found someone who thought the way I did about the important things in life. At about 5 AM my mother, who had been looking for me, found me on the steps of the stage and said in a teasing tone of voice, "I thought you wanted to go home early." I was hoping that he would ask to see me again, but I was not sure of his intensions. The rules require that the man asks. At the last minute he set up a meeting at the subway entrance in front of the Rex for three days later. For three days, it was like I was in a dream. I went about my business like a sleepwalker. When the appointed evening arrived, I was anxious. Maybe I wouldn't recognize him. Maybe I had exaggerated how good-looking he was. But I was not disappointed: he was as handsome as I had envisioned, resembling Louis Jourdan. So for two months we went out regularly. The only thing that surprised me was that he waited two weeks before kissing me. I didn't understand why. He later told me that he wanted to be sure of his feelings, for he had realized that I was a serious young woman and he didn't want to play with my feelings. We loved to dance. We went regularly to the Olympia. We walked a lot. Before I met him I wasn't very athletic. With him, I learned to be. He read poetry to me. He played the harmonica. He introduced me to jazz. We liked the same musicAfter several weeks, my father insisted that we spend the weekend in our cottage in the country in Auchy-La-Montagne, a house that I had urged my father to buy. My mother had hated the countryside since her early childhood. You had to go get water from the well. We went there with the Zingers, and I remember that Mrs. Zinger, knowing that I was dating a young man, tried to convince me that the most important thing in life was one's financial situation, that even if one is in love, after a few years one no longer has anything to say to one's partner. She succeeded in sowing doubts in my mind, forcing me to ask myself: on what was I embarking at the age of eighteen? I had perhaps not made the most of my youth.

When I came back from that weekend, I saw Maurice and he could sense my doubts because he read me like an open book. He forced the issue, saying: "I am getting serious about you, and if you don't feel the same way, then I'd rather break it off now. " At that moment I realized how important he was to me, and I was deeply.. upset at the mere thought of never seeing him again. Indeed, I thought I was a little too young to commit myself, but on the other hand I wasn't going to ruin my future for a few minor concerns. I had realized that he didn't really have a good job. He was a leather craftsman which demanded a lot of skill and talent but wasn't a trade that paid much. My father realized that as well, perhaps, and yet again he tried to make me do what he wanted. I had a date to meet Maurice at 2 PM at the Place des Filles du Calvaire that Sunday. My father decided that I wouldn't go out that day. My parents were redoing the kitchen at the time, which meant that the entrance hall was being used as a kitchen. My mother had tried to persuade me to go tell Maurice (because he didn't have a telephone) that I couldn't go out with him that day, but I refused to submit. Meanwhile my mother had gone down to the workshop to stitch something. I had a confrontation with my father. I refused to give in. Something in me broke at that moment; I could no longer stand this dictator who decided when I could laugh or cry. I began to scream, to tremble, and to hiccup, unable to breathe. My father became frightened, pleading with me to calm down. I was trembling and barely able to stand as my father led me to my bedroom. I lied down and soon fell asleep. Meanwhile, Maurice telephoned from a phone booth because I hadn't shown up. My mother answered and told him that I had gone out with my cousin. He went home completely stunned. He couldn't believe what he had heard, that I, Hélène, the girl he held in such high esteem, had stood him up. His parents and his sister didn't understand what had happened. At first he didn't want to say anything about it to anyone, but his sister was insistent, so Maurice admitted: "Hélène stood me up and went out with a supposed female cousin." His sister couldn't believe it either and after a moment of reflection said to him, "It's impossible. That isn't something Hélène would do. If she wanted to break up with you, she would have told you to your face," and then she added, smiling: "Look, you were a heartbreaker, and now it's your turn to suffer. But take my word for it, if I were in your shoes I would call her and talk things out with her." That episode of hysterics had so worn me out that I slept for the entire afternoon. When I awoke my parents had gone out with those cousins who had come into town from elsewhere. When Maurice telephoned me again, I arranged to see him and we met up like usual at the metro station Filles du Calvaire. What a surprise he had when he saw me: I didn't need to explain a great deal, because my face was swollen from crying. He told me later that the state of my face was the reason he wanted to walk rather than take the metro. I think that I had frightened my father so much that he never tried to impose his authority over me. I think he realized that if he wanted me at his table, he would have to invite Maurice as well. As for me, I loved to go to Maurice's parents' home. I was always made to feel very welcome and after lunch on Sunday we were free to go out for a stroll to Buttes Chaumont or the Champs Élysées. I preferred the latter and Maurice always joked that "I had bourgeois taste" which is true. I always had a taste for luxury, but most of the time I didn't have the financial means to buy luxury goods. I have always liked beautiful things. The summer of 1949 my father had rented an apartment at La Baule-les-Pins for two months. So for the month of July I was in charge, taking care of my two sisters while my parents finished up the production season. I missed Maurice a great deal, but we wrote to each other every day. In August I was surprised to learn that my father invited Maurice to La Baule. He slept on a sofa-bed in the living room with my sister Annette. My parents had the bedroom which adjoined the living area and my sister Françoise and I slept in another bedroom. Maurice didn't have a lot of money so he took all his meals with us, but in the evening around 11 PM, he would take me out to the café on the corner of the Boulevard de l'Océan at La Baule-les-Pins for a cup of coffee and croissants and we talked for hours, philosophizing about life, but we didn't have many illusions about human nature, for we had escaped the Holocaust. Since we had met, the creation of the state of Israel had taken place. It was full of people who had returned from the death camps and who once again were forced to struggle for survival. In my family (for his had largely disappeared), we were all very concerned about Israel. We knew that it was vitally important that the Jews have a land of refuge for when things go badly and that we might one day take refuge in that land which belongs to our history. Today we are hounded by that same hatred. It is stirred up by certain people who make Jews the object of all anger and see such activity as a means of getting power. Still today where there might have been peace in that beautiful country [Israel], there is blood and misery. But what hope do we have when we see that today certain human beings are ready to die in suicide bombings in order to kill others. It's a negation of life. I cannot believe that any mothers are willing to send their children off to commit suicide. It's pure brain-washing. Life should be more precious than anything else; as it is, life is so fragile. It is true that we are privileged to have escaped the massacre, and that those who returned from the camps were marked for the rest of their lives. They will never be able to forget the horrors of the death camps. I have often wondered how the executioners of those camps could survive, but as I already said, they had to have killed their own souls first. One evening coming back home from the café, after drinking another espresso with milk and eating another croissant, we found my sister Annette asleep on the toilet. She had decided that she wanted to wait for us; she liked Maurice a lot. Another evening, I couldn't resist and I went to join Maurice on the sofa, just to snuggle against him. I feared only that my sister would wake up. My father must have heard us whispering, but my mother prevented him from walking in on us, fearing his reaction. When my parents went back to Paris and I stayed on a few days, they had a meeting with Maurice and his parents. They decided, at my father's instigation, the date for our wedding and that Maurice would give up being a leather craftsman and come to work for my father. He held out the prospect of a future full of promise for Maurice in our business. My father was such a smooth talker that he convinced everyone with almost no effort. I must add that Maurice's own mother didn't care for the leather trade. Because of the war, Maurice had had to interrupt his studies, and after the war he had enlisted in the army for 18 months, so when he returned he had to deal with the most urgent matters first and that meant earning a living. Personally, I was not in agreement. I knew my father's character. I didn't want Maurice to fall under his control. I told my father what I thought of his idea, but he said that Maurice would take the place of the son he never had, and he ended up convincing me. The future would prove that I had been right. Maurice became a salesman for our company. Meanwhile there was some suggestion that perhaps Maurice and I might open a small retail shop. We did some research and found something at the Saint Pierre market. There would be some costs attached to taking it over, but my father had asked his friend Jacques who was ready to lend him the money. Then my father changed his mind, thinking that he had to secure his own future, so he began to look for and he found a wholesale shop for himself on the rue Réaumur. It wasn't the ideal place for wholesale in the textile field, but it was better than being on the second floor on the Avenue Ledru Rollin. Thus the beautiful dreams of the "Girl who counted her chickens before they hatched" evaporated before our eyes.

My father had said that Maurice would become his partner, but that too was no more than empty words. I remained under his thumb, and so did Maurice. But when he wanted to, he could be so charming...

# 10 My wedding but no bed of roses

So the date for the wedding was set: July 22, 1950. We began to look for a small apartment. We found one on the Rue au Foin, in the middle of the Marais, and to my way of thinking, it was a neighborhood where we might one day become independent from my father. I just couldn't stand being under his authority any more. All week we worked together and on the weekend he wanted us to go with him to their country cottage in Auchy-La-Montagne. Of course Maurice did not see things the same way. My father had sent him to take driving lessons, and now that he had his driver's license, my father loaned him his car, a large Renault that we had named "Pamela". My father was very different from Maurice's father, a man who had never been ambitious, who loved to read, but wasn't very outgoing. But life did not treat him kindly. He lost his mother when he was very young; his father remarried and then sold their house without giving anything to his son who, in order to survive, had to work all day and study at night in order to get his certificate. He worked for years with his brother, thinking that they were partners, but then found himself out on the street with nothing after an argument. Life had made him withdrawn. He also lost his sister Leah who was picked up in a round-up and never came back. So Maurice's mother had been dazzled by my father and she pushed Maurice to forge ahead with him, whom only I really knew. Without realizing it, she constantly complained to my parents about her husband's lack of ambition. By denigrating her husband, my mother-in-law harmed her son. It also explains why my father didn't respect his son-in-law. Not surprisingly, when I asked my father for the money that I had loaned him to make payments, money that I had saved from my salary in order to pay for the acquisition of the apartment on the Rue au Foin, he claimed that since he had moved his workshop to the Rue Réaumur, we could just move into the old workshop on the Ave Ledru Rollin, which was directly below my parents' apartment. I was not wild with joy at the idea of living right below my father, who could then control us more. But once again, Maurice's mother was dazzled, this time by the amount of space (80.2 square meters), and she urged us to accept. In any event, I didn't have a choice, because my father didn't have the money to give back to me. Then my father encouraged us to buy furniture on credit, because he had to show off to his friends how well his daughter was living, without specifying who had paid for the furniture. The morning of our wedding, I had to do a few more accounts for my father, which resulted in our being late to city hall. In his haste, he almost drove into the wall of the city hall. Our wedding night took place in our workshop apartment. My mother had made double curtains for us, but had measured incorrectly, and they were thus too short. Because neither my parents nor my new in-laws were well-to-do, my trousseau consisted of two pairs of sheets, four pillow cases, six towels, two tablecloths and twelve napkins. We began our married life in debt, with a shaky financial situation, but with much love and even more tenderness, which has always saved us in difficult moments. And we have had difficult moments! It is also true that I had found someone who was multi-talented. From the time we got up in the morning he made me laugh. He was my Charlie Chaplin. The years pass so quickly and life is so short. It has been nineteen years since my father and my husband died. Much has happened, before then and since. I soon realized that my father was jealous of Maurice, and that he would be very strict with him. Every situation was a good opportunity for my father to assert his power and to humiliate Maurice. What my father didn't realize was that the more he tried to prove to me that my husband was worthless, the more I stood by his side, defending him against my father, and the more I grew away from my father, that father whom I once had adored, but who had lost, little by little, all of his halo.

Maurice, in contrast, was the focus of my admiration. He was the best of husbands, full of kind gestures with me, always helping me with the housework. Not having money, we had to decorate the apartment ourselves; we didn't have the means to buy paintings. Maurice, who had never before painted, began to create paintings by copying postcards. I was his muse, because he, like any self-respecting artist, was always critical of his own work. Any number of times, I had to keep him from destroying what he made. So, little by little, our walls were made attractive by Maurice's canvases. My mother asked Maurice to make her a painting which later was hung right in the middle of her dining room. Maurice was very good with his hands, so whenever something needed repairing, my mother always called him, and she spent a lot of time singing his praises. Maurice this and Maurice that, and of course my father took umbrage more and more at this praise. Nevertheless, between fits of jealousy, life went on, with me working for my father as secretary, saleswoman, packager, and Maurice as sales representative. Maurice had ideas, and he had shown my father models of shirts that my father copied; thus Maurice began to develop a strong client base in chic boutiques and orders poured in. Of course it was at precisely that time that my father hired another sales representative for Paris and gave him the list of Maurice's clients. Naturally, the new sales representative tried to secure clients close to those of Maurice. Maurice's clients thought that it was he who had done so, and they got angry. I will remember until the end of my life the scene that transpired in the car that brought us back every day for lunch at Avenue Ledru Rollin, when Maurice reproached my father for having created that situation. My father said that Maurice couldn't tell him what to do, stopped the car, and ordered him to get out. I hated my father at that moment for having humiliated my husband and I promised myself that one day we would no longer be under his heel. But realizing that he would lose his best worker, and with me threatening to leave, my father returned to more positive feelings about Maurice which allowed us to renegotiate our employment agreement, and everything went smoothly for a time. Then he had the idea that Maurice and I should travel all around France to get orders for him. He urged us to buy a car, a used Fiat 500, pushing us into debt again. We accepted, because we really liked the prospect of traveling together. He was supposed to pay part of our expenses. Our trip began in Normandy. Introducing ourselves as a young couple worked to encourage a certain level of indulgence towards us, and we were able to pick up a good number of orders. Then we arrived in La Baule where we made a big client who gave us an order for 200 shirts. But on our way back to the car we noticed that the shop next door was up for sale. We left to prospect Saint Nazaire. We stopped close to a shop that sold mostly sewing supplies, and suddenly I realized that the name of the owner was the same one mentioned on the store for sale in La Baule: La Planche. One couldn't forget a name like that. I suggested to Maurice that we go in and ask the price. Maurice responded: "With what money do you plan to pay for it?" Ever the optimist I suggested that perhaps the owner would give us credit. We asked to speak to the owner and explained the situation. He liked us, because we were a young couple, and he gave us the keys to the store, saying: "Go take a look at it and see if you like it, and then we'll talk about terms." We went back to La Baule: that shop was made for us. It was rustic, adorable, with a little wooden cash box. Everything was miniature, and on the second floor there was a small office, with just enough room for a chair, and windows that looked like hen cages. It was really unconventional, a dream shop. We went back to Saint-Nazaire. Maurice, who was far more practical than I, asked me how we were going to pay for the shop, because we didn't have any money. The owner suggested that we pay him after the season ended, but we still had to come up with 200,000 francs to pay to register the business. Maurice said it was impossible; I said that maybe our parents could help, and that above all we didn't want to miss the opportunity of a lifetime. Hearing that, Maurice found a post office: I telephoned my father who agreed to loan us 100,000 francs and Maurice called his mother who agreed to loan him 100,000 francs. And that was the beginning of the great adventure of our lifetime.

.

# 11 La Baule-the beginning of our freedom

. We completed our trip through France in two weeks. My father would provide the merchandise for the shop and every night we would do the accounting, putting aside in envelopes the money to pay for the merchandise. We managed to stock the Lacoste brand and a certain knit. The Lacoste name helped us get to know the people of La Baule because at the time Lacoste shirts were difficult to find. We were so happy the two of us; there was no one to boss us around, and the neighbors liked us, except for the one who had ordered shirts from us before we saw the shop, an order that we of course canceled. At midday every day we went to the beach. We ate only a sandwich which allowed us the time to go into the water. What a wonderful life. We were friends with a couple in Le Pouliguen who had a costume jewelry shop on the boardwalk. The husband was a buddy of Maurice. They went camping together. She was of British extraction; her parents owned wholesale costume jewelry shops, and that's why the two of them had their own shop. The difference between them and us was that her parents had bought them the shop and gave them the merchandise. For them everything they sold was pure profit. They really didn't have any worries. When business was slow, he would nap while she looked after the store. They really had a strange relationship. She attended to his every need. When she served him dinner, she looked at him with devotion while he ate at top speed; he always said to her: "Mimi it's really good." I had never seen such a devoted wife. Every evening after we closed, at around 8 PM, we went by to visit them. Together we discussed our future, hoping to be successful in our businesses. We had been married for two years at this point, and I thought that maybe we should try to have a baby. At first Maurice was not convinced, but little by little he began to like the idea. So my daughter was conceived in La Baule. We had found an adorable little apartment that opened onto a garden. The only problem was that the owner had cats. The first night was unbearable, we itched all over. The next morning we realized, upon closer inspection, that there were fleas. We had to take drastic measures to rid our place of those little intruders, but other than that, life was good. Every day we took pleasure in doing the books, putting aside the money for the suppliers, and accumulating the money we needed to pay Mr. Laplanche at the end of the season (200,000 francs). It was a dream life for us. At the end of the season we had enough to pay for the place, the suppliers, and to pay back my in-laws. We figured that my father had made a considerable amount off of the sale of his merchandise to us. We returned to Paris when the tourist season was over, I think it was around September 15, 1952. I was pregnant. Of course, we were once more under my father's thumb, because I was once again his secretary and Maurice was his sales representative. After several days of respite, because my father was very happy about becoming a grandfather, the big scene took place. It must have been a Sunday near noon. My father came into our kitchen and abruptly asked me (Maurice was in the kitchen as well, as we were about to eat): "Tell me, can you give me back the 100,000 francs that I loaned you?" I became quite pale, because it was a given that we would pay him back as soon as we were able. I responded "You know that we had to pay Mr. Laplanche; we don't have enough money to pay you back". My father continued to talk only to me and, paying no attention to what I just said, continued: "You could pay me back 50,000 francs." At that moment, Maurice, who had been witness to the entire scene, became upset saying to my father: "Get out of here". My father left, of course, but we knew that it was the end of the good relations with my father. One might wonder why every time I had a confrontation with my father, my mother never intervened. She didn't feel entitled to her say and was afraid of his anger. Through my mother, my father let me know that I was to find my own job, and that it was out of the question that Maurice return to work for him. So from one day to the next we found ourselves without any financial resources. I went off to look for a position as a secretary. My main concern, being two months pregnant, was to find something before anyone suspected my condition. Maurice went back to his old trade as a leather craftsman, and worked for different firms. He had a lot of setbacks, but finally he found a boss, by the name of Covi, who was an angel. So that Maurice would not lose time, Covi would deliver the work to him at home and come to pick up the items when they were ready. My father found a secretary but she didn't suit him. Again using my mother as a go-between, he asked me to come back to work for him, with the understanding that during the high season I could open our shop in La Baule. For a number of reasons and because I was pregnant I accepted his offer, and I sent his secretary to take the job I had found. I did so with regret because the woman boss there was charming and I'm sure I would have been much happier had I stayed there. Once again, I was back living with the same nonsense, with my father doing all he could to "please" me. He told me that when I gave him back his money I had to pay him interest as well. As for the merchandise for our shop, we could no longer buy on approval and send back what didn't sell. Of course, in that case, Maurice and I decided to find suppliers who would help us to build our business with a more high class clientele. Months passed. My father was unaware that Maurice had found work and Maurice asked me not to say anything about it to my parents. In his ignorance, my father, playing the Good Samaritan, asked if I wanted him to talk to Maurice about finding a job, as though my husband were lazy. My mother was very wise; she wasn't well educated; she could only read Yiddish, but she had so much good sense. She hated arguments and would say to me: "you don't get along with your father because you have the same personality". But what I couldn't bear was injustice, and my father was injustice incarnate. Between two storms, things returned to fair weather. Our relationship improved, and again my father tried to monopolize our weekends. I awaited the birth of my baby. Once or twice, when Maurice passed by the shop, he found me on a stepladder. He told my father in no uncertain terms how dangerous this could be for me. Then my father chastised me for not calling someone to help me when I needed shirt boxes from high shelves. But of course when I was taking care of a client, it was difficult to call for someone else in the middle of a sale. While waiting for the birth of the baby, we sometimes went out on Sunday afternoons with our friend from La Baule to the Bois de Vincennes. She too was pregnant. One day, just before going out, I slipped on my too-well waxed floor and fell flat on my back. Not feeling hurt, I didn't go to see the doctor. Nevertheless, I was two weeks late for my delivery. I worked until the last day. That evening, we had gone to the movies, and the only thing that I remember was that a baby was born in the film. We went home after the film, I went to bed, and an hour later the pains started. I asked Maurice to take me to the hospital. "Are you sure you can't wait until tomorrow morning?" And I answered, "No certainly not!" Maurice called the hospital that wasn't expecting me on that day and was full up. So, despite the fact that we had a reservation there, there was no room for me and I had to go to another hospital where my obstetrician also worked. I don't remember his name; he was a Professor who had been recommended. Because of my fall, the baby was in a breech position, having turned. Labor lasted 17 hours, and I was completely exhausted when I finally gave birth. Restoration work was being done on that hospital and during labor I had to listen to nonstop hammer blows. My parents were in my room. My father spent his time sponging my forehead. With all those people around me, I couldn't scream which might have been a relief. Seeing me suffer so, Maurice promised to never again get me pregnant. I ended up asking them all to leave the room. What a relief when they put the mask over my face in order to put me to sleep and I no longer felt anything. When I woke up, I saw my baby with her almond-shaped eyes and a tiny little nose. The professor said to me that it was a girl and I answered that my father would be disappointed; he really wanted a grandson because he had three daughters. The professor was surprised by my answer and asked Maurice: "And what did you want?" He answered that he didn't care, that what mattered was that it was over. Then the professor turned to me and said "Look how beautiful she is!" I answered that she looked Chinese, and he said: "You don't know anything; she's a real beauty. It was true: she was a true little doll. The next day the professor came to see me and he gave me a book "Au bon beurre", saying that after all I had suffered, I deserved to laugh a little. I was very touched that this important professor had gone to the trouble of coming to see me and bringing me this book. Maurice was supposed to take care of the official acts at city hall, and right after the birth he had made a list of first names that he liked and read them to me: "Catherine, Caroline, Christine" and without thinking I chose Christine, reminded of a film I had liked, La Reine Christine with Greta Garbo. The choice was scandalous because Christine was a purely Catholic name, and not ideal for a little Jewish girl. In his disapproval, my father gave the baby a bracelet with the name "Suzanne" engraved on it. Suzanne had been the name of his mother. My daughter never wore it. In the end we named her Christine and for years it didn't bother us. Later when we came back to Paris and my daughter starting dating boys from the Jewish community, it posed a few problems, because some of them refused to believe that she was Jewish. She was born on April 9th, and naturally her arrival completely changed our lives. First we dealt with the constant succession of nursemaids. I had to go to work. For the first few weeks I breast fed, but unfortunately she didn't take too much milk. I could have fed half a dozen babies. My milk was too rich; she didn't digest it well, so after a few weeks Christine was put on the bottle. That allowed me to go back to work. Because her father worked at home, he could supervise the nursemaid. But the first one, who was perfect, only stayed with us for three weeks and then suddenly decided that she wanted to be a stewardess. The second came from Alsace. She took good care of the cooking and the house, but one day Maurice found the baby in the middle of the smoky kitchen and fired her immediately. Meanwhile, we had to prepare for our shop season. We contacted several famous companies: bathing suits from Jantzen, Lacoste, Bril pants, and an Italian knitwear company. Of course we no longer could get merchandise on approval, so we were looking at more risk. We had to pay the suppliers and absorb what did not sell, but we were full of confidence. Things wouldn't be easy but we were so happy to be going off to La Baule. We had rented a small apartment next door to the shop, and would be able to keep an eye on the shop from our window. My sister Françoise was supposed to come for one month during the season to help us out. Some time in June, we, the baby, and the suitcases set out for La Baule. We set up a little hammock across the inside of the train compartment for the baby. Christine was an adorable baby; she never cried, and the trip went very smoothly. The other passengers were charmed that she was so little trouble. Maurice had to stop his leather work for the summer. His boss called him "my seasonal worker" and accepted that he stop during June and return in September. At the beginning of September we had a clearance sale, and that allowed us to liquidate what hadn't sold. We had cots on which we placed the merchandise. It was a pedestrian street, and we had a really good time that day. The confectioner Manuel from across the street took a liking to us, along with the shoemaker and their son Jean-Pierre. I also became friends with Eres who had a shoe store on the Avenue General De Gaulle. They had all come as clients and became friends. As well as the lawyer and his wife, the owner of the Peugeot car dealership, the famous brothers who were builders, the owners of a well known fitness center and sailing club, the insurance agent. They all knew each other, of course, for they had been in La Baule for years. Most of them played golf and tennis, and were the jet set of La Baule. We were surprised that they were so friendly towards us. I suppose that we were a change from the usual routine. We only came in the summer, we were from Paris, we were different from them (we were Jewish with the burden of all that past on our shoulders). In fact, we never told anyone we were Jewish. Maurice and I had been so traumatized by the yellow star we had to wear during the Occupation that we wanted to avoid possible anti-Semitism, which is deeply ingrained in our society. We wanted to be judged on our acts and our behavior alone, but at the end of the day, maybe it was no secret, and we were the only ones who didn't know that they were perfectly aware of our background. It didn't matter; we found in that group of people a great deal of consideration and friendship. When we returned we paid my father back the 100.000 francs that we owed him. The next year my parents came to La Baule on vacation, but didn't understand that we weren't free during the season. That we had to sell as much as possible, that the tourist season was short. One day they took Christine to the beach; it was very windy that day and Maurice went to get her because he was concerned that she might catch a cold. This made my father angry. It was the story of his life to be angry at us. Every year our sales got bigger, but then we suffered a blow. We had a three-year lease, but the landlord refused to renew it; he wanted to rent to us only for the tourist season, but we knew that with a three-year lease we had control over the commercial property. We had to go to court, and my father told us, haughtily:" When one doesn't have money you can't defend yourself", but we weren't about to let the whole enterprise go. Luckily, as our lawyer said to us, "justice is flexible", so that gave us until 1958. His pretext for wanting the shop back was that, unable to get along with his wife, he needed a place to live. If he had won, he would have paid us 300,000 francs, but in fact the whole matter cost us 400,000 francs. He claimed that he always won in the Saint Nazaire court, but we appealed to the Rennes court. Maurice went to take photos of his luxurious property. Meanwhile he was sleeping in the shop next door which he had taken back from a young couple who had chosen not to defend their rights. We were living with that sword of Damocles over our heads, but we were prepared to fight. Meanwhile we still didn't like the workshop-apartment we inhabited just below my parents. Luckily for us, the landlord of the Avenue Ledru Rollin place wanted to set up a new lease provided he received the arrears on the rent based on the new amount, something like 3,000 francs. My father didn't want to pay that sum, and therefore decided to put the lease in our names provided we pay it. We accepted to do it so we owned the lease on a mixed commercial property that could also serve as a residence. Later my friend Eres bought a shop in Saint Nazaire. She took me there to see it. Another shop not far from hers was for rent. It had a lovely apartment on the fourth floor, a view of the Saint Nazaire port from the kitchen. We could look out and see them build the liner France. We decided to take it, not realizing that it was in a bad spot. While it was on the main thoroughfare, it was next door to a shirt-maker, a really Breton, who would make us suffer. It was a turning point in our lives, and we had to find someone to take our apartment. Of course when we told the news to our parents, they were far from happy. One day when we went by my parents' place, my father accused Maurice of having planned to separate us from our family and, among other choice comments, said: "you stole the pearl of the family and now you want to separate her from us". Maurice, who was always philosophical about these matters, responded: "It was up to you to keep her". Obviously this was all nonsense, and it was only my father's authoritarian character that had alienated me. And it was I who had pushed Maurice to make the deal in Saint Nazaire. In any case, we needed to be out there to conduct our defense against the landlord of the La Baule shop. We won in the Rennes court of appeal. I had gone there and I was supposed to just listen, but luckily I was fearless. At the hearing I spoke out and asked the judge to look at the photos that Maurice had taken of the luxurious property that our landlord owned. The judge looked at them while telling me to be quiet, because normally, as my lawyer had told me, I didn't have the right to speak, but we won our case. The court awarded us three million francs, as opposed to the 300,000 that the landlord wanted to give us. It was a great victory. What we didn't realize was that there was a deadline for vacating the place, in this case June 25th. We thought we were going to be able to stay through the tourist season. We had brought in all the merchandise. Of course the lawyer hadn't said anything about this matter. Three days before the deadline for vacating a bailiff arrived and gave us a formal notice to vacate the premises on June 25th, indicating that after that date, each day we remained would cost us a penalty of 1% of the compensation per day, which meant that at the end of 100 days we would have lost the entire compensation, and we'd still have to give up the keys. So Maurice had to move all of the merchandise in three days. I helped him in the evening, because during the day I was at the Saint Nazaire shop. People couldn't understand why we were moving right before the beginning of the tourist season. They thought we were crazy. So after a race against the clock, with the store finally empty, we wanted to turn the keys over to the landlord, but he wouldn't accept them, because he wanted his shop in exactly the state in which he had rented it.

Maurice had to find a team to pull out the racks and showcases. The whole thing took three days. We were desperate; we were looking at the destruction of all our hopes. The landlord was radiant. He had played a trick on us of his own devising, and at the end he said: "In any case you won't find anything for that amount of money." As I mentioned earlier, our client-friends at La Baule liked us a lot. One of them, the attorney, called to tell us that an occupied store was for sale, and that the tenant was at the end of his lease. So we bought the building and offered the tenant compensation to free the premises early. He was the same kind of person as our landlord. Despite the fact that he didn't make good business, and for the good reason that he was selling wool for knitting with a coal-burning stove dating back to Methuselah in the middle of the room. So we had to take him to court, and it took six years to evict him and to give him his compensation. So in 1961 we had a shop in Saint Nazaire where we didn't do much business, full of the stock from the La Baule shop where, despite our signs indicating everything was on sale, we were not successful in selling the stock from La Baule. We were owners of a shop that wasn't free. It was a real catastrophe for our finances. Maurice was completely worn out from all the work he had to do. I urged him to leave for a few days togo see our daughter who was at Auchy La Montagne, my parents' country cottage, where my aunt Guenia and her children were there as well. Her twins loved to tease Christine which they could do because she was much younger than they were. My mother-in-law had gone to see her granddaughter and she quickly caught on to what the twins were doing. They had to read Les Misérables and Christine was for them Cosette. Her grandmother's vigilance rectified the situation. In any case Maurice thought his mother overestimated the problem and that the twins gave Christine some company. After a long weekend he came back to Saint Nazaire, and one evening after returning from the cinema, I had the idea to go look in the mailbox at 11 PM. There was a little note from the attorney telling us that the shop across from our store in La Baule was free to rent for the season. Because the woman who had been a tenant for many years (we called her Kodak), who spent all her time drinking and insulting clients from her doorstep, had been thrown out by the landlord and he was ready to rent the shop to us for the season, a season that was well under way, mind you; it was July 12th. We rented the shop. In three days we, or rather Maurice, repainted it gray. We went back and forth from Saint Nazaire to La Baule to bring back the merchandise and on July 15th the store opened, the windows were set up and we remained open that season until 11 PM every evening. The attorney and his wife came over to compliment us on our courage. Indeed, we needed a miracle to succeed, and the good fortune of finding this store allowed to us to land on our feet. An angel must have been watching over us. After the tourist season, the same attorney friend helped us once again. He found a store that was across from the property, which we owned.  The tenant, who was old, wanted to sell his lease. The attorney found us a lender to mortgage the walls of our property. When we opened this new shop we realized that this would finally be the chance of our lives. The site was first class, with the shop, the kitchen, the back of the shop, all looking out on a courtyard that we shared with the owner of a coffee shop well known for their famous pastries, with whom we had become friends. During the off-season, Maurice played tennis with him. Everyone called us Mr. and Mrs. Peggy, because Peggy was the name of our store. We quickly realized that the two of us did not suffice as salespeople. We hired some personnel; first students for the tourist season and then full time. We also evolved in our choice of merchandise. We became the authorized dealer for Rodier knits, Bril pants and jackets, Luisa Spagnoli knits, Pancaldi shirts, Yves St Laurent ties. These joined our mascot brand Lacoste. We put in our orders in the winter. The sales representatives came to see us. Most became friends. 1964 was the highpoint. We opened the shop of our dreams, after recovering the property we owned across the street. It was a real mess! We had to redo everything: one of our client friends rebuilt the whole store including adding a second floor. That gave us double the space: 100 square meters. The counters were Louis XVI chests of drawers, and there was a real office for us. We realized our dreams of a luxurious store. In 1964, another client-friend, a builder, helped us buy an apartment on the edge of the sea at Baule-les-pins, a corner apartment with a view of the bay, a real dream. We didn't have the money to buy it, but he found a friend willing to give us the down payment. I had learned that the best way to borrow was through the banks, and that when you own the building, you will always be able to find money.

# 12 Versailles- A new adventure

In 1968 we saw in the newspaper that they were going to build a large shopping center near Versailles. "Parly II" was one of the first shopping centers, built on the model of the American mall. Despite our commercial success, we missed our families and the friends we still had in Paris and whom we saw only during our winter sports vacations. Our families we saw only for the Jewish holidays. I saw too that our daughter was very lonely, in part for the good reason that she wasn't Catholic and thus didn't attend church, and as I noted earlier, we were not from the same world as our client-friends. We really didn't have a social life. So we took the first steps towards returning to the Paris area. The shopping center Parly II wasn't right for us because we would have had to spend a fortune to build the shop and then pay a rent of 7% of what we took in, with an exorbitant minimum rent. In another ad we found for sale a shop under construction in Versailles Grand Siècle, which included 1000 apartments and a shopping center. In our mind it was just an investment for later on. The builder contacted us and after negotiations, because he really needed a place to market the apartments, he paid us 1,200 francs a month and built the shop, for it was an unfinished shell. We gave him a 24-month lease, for we had learned at our own expense not to give him commercial property, and at the end of the lease he would give us back the shop and all of his work, with no further compensation. After the two years, he needed an extension of 12 months, and we set up a new lease in the bank's name for the same reason of not wanting to risk giving away commercial property, and it wound up being the biggest deal of our lives. Grand Siècle was a magnificent achievement. In 1972 we bought an apartment with incredible terms for the loan, because, meanwhile, we had sold the lease of the store near the bakery, to somebody who wanted to open a bookstore that also sold newspapers. It was too complicated to have two shops. After the fantastic level of sales that we had in the new store, the situation went downhill little by little: competitors set up shop only for the tourist season, and the tourists bought cheaper fashion; not high quality. So while during the tourist season our shop was always full, we nonetheless had a drop in business despite all the people who passed by. In the business world it is very important to keep one's eyes open and to not blame unfavorable circumstances for the fact that our sales were not improving. We had to completely change our buying strategy, especially for women, because men are more conservative. Every two weeks I went to Paris to buy the latest trends in women's fashion and we soon saw the difference in our sales. As soon as the packages were opened, the merchandise flew off the shelves, but at the same time we accumulated the stock that had been ordered in advance. All those trips were tiresome. In 1972 we opened the shop in Versailles and moved to the apartment in Versailles. We decided that during the winter the main saleswoman would be in charge with her sister and that we would be there for Easter, Pentecost, and from June to September. That would allow me to do the buying and to not have to order too far in advance. In 1974 we decided to sell the apartment in La Baule which no longer served any function. Our daughter was happy to live in Versailles as she had made friends in the Jewish community. She had rediscovered her roots. Things being what they were, life was not ideal: Maurice and I were often separated during that period and we had to find a solution. In 1972 Maurice's mother became sick. She had that terrible illness which is the plague of humanity. When this happens in a family it changes the whole world, because it is so sad to see those you love deteriorate little by little and not be able to do anything for them. You see the despair in the eyes of a loved one, and it's intolerable. When a loved one dies suddenly, you don't have time to see them suffer. There are two worlds: one of people in good health who think themselves invincible and one where the sick find themselves in the hospital where healthy people take care of them. And most of the time they receive the indifference of those in good health.

Maurice's mood after the death of his mother went downhill, and, as he put it so well, "one is all alone under one's skin," and no one can help you. Maurice's father, who had always been very silent, became more and more taciturn. He missed this woman terribly, despite the fact that she was the opposite of him, excessive in everything, going straight from laughter to tears. In 1976 we decided to rent out the shop in La Baule and our friend the attorney found us a group of builders who were going to build a Marina. We were supposed to rent the shop for the year, which would have allowed us to keep ownership of the building, but at the last minute they offered to buy the building. With what we know now we realized that we should not have accepted; it was too little and on top of that they wanted it before the month of July, which meant that we didn't have it for the entire tourist season. Maurice's father had also come down with that awful disease. We could not resist. Maurice had warned me, "You want to return to the Paris region, but life is not as simple there as here, where we are well known." In Paris there is such competition that it is difficult to make a place for oneself in the sun. He was right, but I also was tired of this life where I had to work seven days a week, with no vacation or very little. I wanted to live, to make the most of life, to have vacations like everyone else, to travel. Christine was ready to get married. Maurice did not really have feelings with his future son-in-law, but it was the choice of his daughter. I would say that it is always difficult for a father, who wants the best for his daughter, to accept a stranger. My father-in-law died in 1976. He never met the husband of his granddaughter. He always said, when speaking of us, that Maurice and I had succeeded in life because we always got along. 1977- Christine was married and we thought it would be for better and for worse. My daughter and my son-in-law went into the real estate business with our help and his parents. I had found a good site because of my habit of reading the personal ads. We took care of fixing up the place, which consisted of a shop on the ground floor and a cute, little apartment on the second floor, in the St. Louis district of Versailles. Maurice had not thought it a good idea from the start. He wanted our daughter to open a little costume jewelry store. 1978- We realized that the Versailles store did not allow us to make enough to live on. Once again we followed the lead of a personal ad that I had found in the newspaper; looking at the map of Paris, we thought we had found our salvation. The next morning we went to see the owner who had already committed to a buyer (true or false), so we offered him more money above his price. Of course, like usual, we did not have a penny and we had to borrow money from our son-in-law to buy this store. Since we bought the building, it was easy for us to find money from banks. Then we borrowed against the apartment in order to pay to have work done on it. We found ourselves in a lot of debt. I can tell you today we had to be super optimistic, but really we didn't have a choice. What saved us a little was that I had the idea to put up signs in the Versailles store that we were closing permanently and that the liquidation of the merchandise would start on August 27th, and so for three weeks people saw the sign. Maurice again warned me that in the month of August there wouldn't even be a cat in our shop. We put all items on sale for a 30% discount. Certain items dated back to the previous year and we had them marked down 50% then, but human nature is incomprehensible. Liquidation always had more of an impact than a sale. To sum up, Maurice had gone down to the store around 8:30am and he had told me, "You've got time; I don't think I'm going to be overwhelmed." At 9:00am he cried for help; hardly had he opened than clients rushed into the shop. When I arrived Maurice was barely visible in the crowd. I had to stand on a stool and ask everyone to go outside and form a line. But we needed help; we had to have someone at the door to stop the customers. We thought that our daughter could help us, but our son-in-law offered to do it and he was perfect because he was very tall, so he was able to dominate the situation. Maurice and I spent the day selling. That night the store was almost empty and my toes hurt. In three days all the merchandise was liquidated. What a success! We couldn't get over it! This store, where we had had so much difficulty making money, had a grand finale. The new store was almost ready. Being in a prestigious district, we were afraid of opening a simple store. Our principal supplier had a license for the brand Pierre Balmain. We signed a contract and became a Pierre Balmain store, for men. The day before the opening we had a reception and Pierre Balmain came in person. The store was splendid, we had a decorator dress the windows, and everything was perfection. The next day, which was a Saturday, we opened the store thinking to see some customers, but no, not a single customer passed through the door. That evening we were devastated. Maurice, while pulling down the metal grating, said to me, "I may as well shoot myself." I also had a heavy heart. What was going to happen to us with all our debts? I tried to analyze the situation and I realized that maybe given that we were a designer store people were intimidated and didn't dare come in. Fortunately, Monday we had a big customer who bought a lot of merchandise. But after two years, we cancelled our contract and the name became "Pierre Edouard." Things went better, but the amount of business was not sufficient. This district had been an illusory seduction for us. In the meantime, we had made a habit of going to the United States for our vacations, where my sister Viviane (Françoise) and her husband Barry lived. They had asked us over the years to come visit, but Maurice did not want to take a plane. We really fell in love with America and Americans. We loved their mentality. If we could have we would have emigrated, but it was too late, or at any rate it was too late for Maurice. He always told me that he had dreamed of marrying an American. 1979- Our grandson Daniel came into the world. This was a huge joy, but my daughter was very tired from the labor. My daughter and I found a little house right on the water in Trouville that they bought. This meant that we could see them on weekends, since we had our little duplex above Deauville in Touregeville. We had our moments of peace where we could make the most of family reunions. In 1984 my father had a prostate operation and while visiting him Maurice, who had problems urinating, consulted my father's surgeon who advised him to have a prostate operation. The surgeon told me that he had cancer, but advised me not to say anything to Maurice, who for three years received treatment, but without knowing what he had. I decided to sell the business and to keep ownership, which allowed us to pay off all our debts and to have an income with the rent payments we received. For three years Maurice's illness was stable. At first I cried every day and then I reasoned with myself that I needed to make the most of the time we had left. We continued to go see Viviane and Barry for our vacation. We went together several times to Florida, California, Bermuda and the last time to Miami in Florida. After our return from vacation, the surgeon wanted Maurice to start radiation and I did not want to take responsibility for making the decision. The surgeon had to tell Maurice the truth. After the first radiation session, Maurice found himself paralyzed and the illness gained more and more ground. In January of 1987 my father also fell ill. He had liver cancer. Things went quickly downhill. In May of 1987 my father died, and Maurice called him a "poor    guy" and he forgave him for all the suffering he had had to endure at my father's hands. Maurice died in July of 1987. My daughter divorced, several months after the death of her father. My daughter asked me to bury her father in Jerusalem where he rests on the Mount of Olives. My younger sister Annette and her husband Marcel came to the funeral and so did my grandson who was eight years old and adored his grandfather. Today I live in the United States. When I went to visit my sister to take my mind off things, I met my second husband Howard. It has been sixteen years since we married. My daughter got remarried to a rabbi three years ago, and I wish with all my heart that she find happiness and peace. Nothing is easy, and life is a perpetual struggle to find a bit of happiness. Nothing is ever definitively acquired. We do our best to reach bliss and when we think that it has come, new ordeals await us. However, I am still, despite everything, an incorrigible optimist who still believes in her future despite being 77 years old; I still make lots of plans. These lines are dedicated to all whom I loved, whom I love, and whom I will love. May all who spend their life hating, losing the very essence of life that should be so precious to everyone.

# Pictures before the war

My Parent's Wedding in Poland

Me at Three Years old in the Jardin des Tullieries Paris

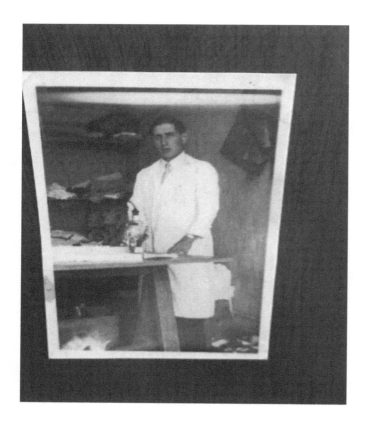

My father in His Workshop Paris

My Father touring France by bicycle

My Father with His Parents at the Cemetery Lodz Poland 1937

# Pictures During the war

Me and My Two Sisters Castelculier (L.G) Free Zone 1943

My Father in the Beaune La Rolande Internment Camp 1941

# Pictures Post War Teenage Years

Teenage Years

My Wedding Day Paris 1950

# Pictures Married Life

Me and My Daughter in La Baule 1955

Me, My Husband and Daughter Eiffel Tower Paris 1960

Me and My Family in the Bois de Vincennes 1981

## Me and My Grandson Versailles 1981

# The Passion of Life: Escaping the Holocaust

My Two Sisters, Me and My Parents

Me, My Daughter and My Grandson in front of my house Versailles 1988

Me, My Mother, My Sister and Grandson in my garden Versailles 1988

Made in the USA
Columbia, SC
06 April 2021